THE NEW ELK HUNTER'S COOKBOOK
AND MEAT CARE GUIDE

THE NEW ELK HUNTER'S COOKBOOK
AND MEAT CARE GUIDE

A collection of favorite recipes and essays from
members of the Rocky Mountain Elk Foundation

SECOND EDITION

ThreeForks™

GUILFORD, CONNECTICUT
HELENA, MONTANA

AN IMPRINT OF THE GLOBE PEQUOT PRESS

Copyright © 2004 by The Globe Pequot Press
A previous edition of this book was published by Falcon Publishing, Inc. in 1994
First Lyons Press edition, 2005

The Lyons Press is an imprint of The Globe Pequot Press.

10 9 8 7 6 5 4 3 2

Printed in the United States of America

Text design: Nancy Freeborn
Interior photos: © Hugh Hogle Photo Collection of the Rocky Mountain Elk Foundation, except for the photographs on pages 224–25, © DusanSmetana.com
Front cover photo: © DusanSmetana.com
Back cover photo: © Hugh Hogle Collection of the Rocky Mountain Elk Foundation

Library of Congress Cataloging-in-Publication Data

The new elk hunter's cookbook and meat care guide : a collection of favorite recipes from members of the Rocky Mountain Elk Foundation.
    p. cm.
  Includes index.
  ISBN 0-7627-2863-9
  1. Cookery (Game) 2. Cookery (Elk) 3. Game and game-birds, Dressing of. I Rocky Mountain Elk Foundation.

TX751.N45 2004
641.6'91—dc22

                                                                    2003060676

Text pages printed on recycled paper

CONTENTS

FOREWORD

There are zillions of cookbooks in kitchens all over America. Each has recipes that are worthy of trying, but very few have as many superb recipes as you'll find in *The New Elk Hunter's Cookbook and Meat Care Guide*. Whether you have a taste for fish, fowl, venison, salad, soup, or dessert, it's all here, and then some.

As one who loves to cook wild game, I'm always eager to peruse new cookbooks and try new recipes. I did just that with this book, and I made some delightful discoveries. Take Phyllis Speer's Elk Henley in Puffed Pastry. If this doesn't make you a hit in your neighborhood, nothing will. The recipe is easy to follow, like most in this book, and is a culinary masterpiece. I can't wait to try others.

Besides recipes, you'll find valuable information on how to store, transport, and care for meat in the field. This is just as important as cooking it, since game that isn't properly taken care of in the woods will never taste great, no matter what magical recipes you try in the kitchen.

I'm mighty glad the Rocky Mountain Elk Foundation had the wisdom to produce this cookbook. It'll be on the shelf closest to the stove in my kitchen, because I'll be using it a lot. I bet you will, too.

JIM ZUMBO, *Outdoor Life* Hunting Editor
Member, Board of Directors, Rocky Mountain Elk Foundation

PREFACE

You may own or have heard of our original *Elk Hunter's Cookbook,* a collection of favorite recipes from members of the Rocky Mountain Elk Foundation, which came out in 1994. The all-time top-selling book the Elk Foundation ever published, it's now nearly out of print. The book you're looking at is entirely new and different. All these recipes still came from RMEF members, and some may be a lot like those in the original book, but that's where the similarities end.

The old cookbook is good, but this one is better. With more than 270 all-new recipes, an informative essay on Dutch oven cooking and another on building a smokehouse, a commentary about the economy of wild game meat, six articles on meat care, and a host of tips on efficient and satisfying food preparation, *The New Elk Hunter's Cookbook and Meat Care Guide* has to be one of the most comprehensive and helpful works ever published for achieving culinary pleasure with wild game meat— and it's written especially for hunters.

The texture and flavor of wild meat can be varied, to say the least. One bad experience can turn a person against it for a lifetime. How sad, for the difference between wild game meat and commercial pork, beef, and poultry can be as great as the difference between strong, rich, fresh-ground, fresh-roasted coffee and the emaciated product that comes in cans. Or between leather and vinyl. Good wild meat is no more expensive than bad wild meat. It's all in the preparation, and there is no good excuse for bad experiences with wild meat at the dinner table. Excellence should and can be the norm. This book will show hunters, outfitters, meat-cutters, and chefs how to achieve it.

It also features recipes for everything from soup to dessert. The whole enchilada. We trust you'll find it useful.

DON BURGESS, *Bugle* Hunting Editor

ABOUT THE ROCKY MOUNTAIN ELK FOUNDATION

The Rocky Mountain Elk Foundation is a nonprofit wildlife conservation organization with an emphasis on elk and elk country. Founded in 1984, RMEF is headquartered in Missoula, Montana. Its members, in 50 states and 23 countries, are dedicated to the foundation's mission to ensure the future of elk and other wildlife and their habitat by
- conserving, restoring, and enhancing natural habitats;
- promoting the sound management of wild, free-ranging elk and other wildlife and their habitat;
- fostering cooperation among federal, state, and private organizations and individuals in wildlife management and habitat conservation; and
- educating members and the public about habitat conservation, the value of hunting, hunting ethics, and wildlife management.

The Elk Foundation advocates sustainable, ethical use of resources and seeks common ground among stakeholders. RMEF celebrates outdoor and rural lifestyles and values within a North American culture growing ever more distant from the land. RMEF's top priority—preventing and offsetting habitat loss—hasn't changed since the organization was founded. The foundation protects and enhances crucial elk habitat including winter range, summer range, migration corridors, and calving grounds, on both private and public lands. Subdivision and development are the major consumers of habitat. RMEF meets the habitat conservation challenge on private lands by negotiating land acquisitions, trades, and conservation easements with willing landowners.

As of 2003, RMEF and its partners have helped enhance or permanently protect nearly 3.7 million acres in the United States—an area 70 percent larger than Yellowstone National Park. Total fundraising has exceeded $446 million. Membership reached a record 138,000 in 2002, including 10,000 volunteers working in 550 chapters and 140 paid staff.

To help the Rocky Mountain Elk Foundation leave an elk country legacy for future generations, visit www.elkfoundation.org or call 1–800–CALL ELK.

Stoking Up Prodigiously

BY DAN CROCKETT

These recipes would have suited Theodore Roosevelt's tastes well. When Roosevelt set out from camp for two or three days' hunting, he carried only a loaf of frying-pan bread or perhaps an elk tongue. But when he sat down at a table, Roosevelt could easily devour a whole chicken or half a suckling pig. His friend Lloyd Griscom described Roosevelt's gourmandizing as "stoking up prodigiously—as though he were a machine." Theodore Roosevelt Jr. allowed as how his father's coffee cup "was more in the nature of a bathtub."

Some of the recipes in *The New Elk Hunter's Cookbook and Meat Care Guide* create treats light and simple enough to slip into one corner of Roosevelt's saddle bags. But most of the dishes set forth on these pages could star in the kind of gastronomic fantasy our hard-riding, hard-hunting, twenty-sixth president might have entertained while riding back toward the cooktent on some long-ago hunting expedition.

Although few of us get to hunt elk for more than a week or two each fall, we are elk hunters throughout the year. Our appetites for elk country, for hunting, and for the elk themselves remain undiminished. Savoring the kind of hearty meal we might eat in elk camp—or at least dream about while gnawing on a piece of jerky—is a fine way to keep those appetites keen. So we asked 140,000 friends of ours if they knew any good recipes.

All the recipes in this book come from people who love elk and elk country. They shared these dishes in the spirit you might swap tall tales and favorite recipes over a low cooking fire. We at RMEF hope a few of these recipes will find their way into your elk camp. We hope you'll cook them at home, too—and the aromas will carry you back to a dawn at timberline, with 3 inches of fresh snow. Most of all, we hope they will make you want to stoke up prodigiously.

Dan Crockett has been the editor of Bugle *magazine since 1992.*

APPETIZERS
AND SOUPS

WILD GAME COCKTAIL MEATBALLS

4 slices white bread

1 cup milk

3 pounds ground venison, moose, elk, or caribou

1 tablespoon garlic powder

1½ tablespoons seasoned salt (such as Lawry's)

¾ tablespoon pepper

4 tablespoons minced onion flakes

1 tablespoon oregano

1 tablespoon paprika

½ teaspoon cinnamon

3 eggs

Tear bread into pieces and cover with milk in a large bowl. Add remaining ingredients and mix thoroughly. Shape into 1-inch balls. Place on jelly-roll pan and bake at 300°F for 20 minutes.

COCKTAIL SAUCE

¼ cup butter

2 medium onions, chopped fine

¼ cup flour

3 cups beef broth

1 cup red wine

¼ cup brown sugar

¼ cup ketchup

2 tablespoons lemon juice

6–8 gingersnaps, crumbled fine

2 teaspoons salt

Pepper to taste

Melt butter. Add onions and sauté until soft. Blend in flour. Add broth and stir until smooth. Add remaining ingredients. Stir to dissolve brown sugar.

Add baked meatballs and simmer 10–15 minutes. Let cool and place in refrigerator for 24 hours (or at least overnight). Reheat before serving.

MARY ANNE LECCE
Collinsville, Illinois

PARTY ELK SNACKS

1–2 pounds of elk or any other large game (¾-inch steaks or
   roasts work best)
1 cup vermouth (we prefer dry, but sweet works)
½ cup bourbon (whiskey or rum work, too)
¼ cup soy sauce
⅛ cup Worcestershire sauce
1 tablespoon coarsely ground pepper
1 tablespoon garlic salt
2 tablespoons dried onion flakes and/or dried parsley flakes
½ pound country bacon, sliced
2 cups flour

On morning of event cut meat into cubes 1–2 inches square by ¾–1 inch thick.
Remove tallow, fat, and gristle. Prepare marinade by mixing vermouth, bourbon, soy
sauce, Worcestershire sauce, pepper, garlic salt, and onion/parsley flakes.

Place meat in a deep bowl with lid and immerse in marinade for 5–8 hours at
room temperature. Add cold water as needed to cover meat. Stir well every 2–3 hours
(may prepare prior evening if refrigerated).

After guests arrive, have consumed some wine or cocktails, and are ready for a
snack, remove the meat from the marinade and place on some paper towels to
absorb excess liquid. Heat a skillet (preferably cast iron) and quickly fry bacon. While
frying, put flour in a paper bag and then shake dried meat in bag to coat (flour in
bowls also works). After bacon is crisp, remove from skillet, reserving the grease.
Quickly put floured meat in skillet and fry until done to your liking. Place meat on
platter or tray with a toothpick in each piece and serve.

BILL AND EV HOFFMAN
Mukilteo, Washington

VENISON CHIP DIP

½ pound ground venison
1 tablespoon seasoned salt
¼ teaspoon ground cumin
¼ tablespoon pepper
¼ tablespoon garlic powder
1 4-ounce can green chiles, diced
1 large tomato, chopped
1 pound processed cheese
½ cup sliced black olives
1 red bell pepper, diced
⅓ cup sliced green onions

Add seasonings to ground venison and fry until done. Add green chiles and half the tomato. Lower heat. Add cheese. Stir until smooth and creamy. Top with remaining tomato, olives, bell pepper, and green onions. Serve with tortilla chips.

JIM WEBER
Helena, Montana

BAMBI BITS

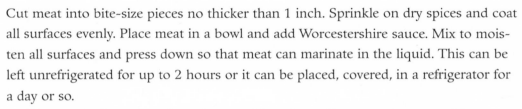

1 pound venison, elk, antelope, or other game meat

1–1½ teaspoons or more creole seasoning (such as Tony Chachere's)

½–¾ teaspoon or more Chef Paul Prudhomme's Meat Magic
    (or other brand of seasoning)

½–1 teaspoon garlic salt

Unflavored meat tenderizer (optional)

½–1 teaspoon lemon pepper (optional)

2–5 tablespoons Worcestershire sauce (or soy sauce)

Bacon slices, cut into 2–3-inch pieces

Cut meat into bite-size pieces no thicker than 1 inch. Sprinkle on dry spices and coat all surfaces evenly. Place meat in a bowl and add Worcestershire sauce. Mix to moisten all surfaces and press down so that meat can marinate in the liquid. This can be left unrefrigerated for up to 2 hours or it can be placed, covered, in a refrigerator for a day or so.

Wrap each piece of marinated meat with a piece of bacon and secure with a wooden toothpick. Grill at high heat for no longer than 5 minutes. Turn once and grill for about another 3 minutes. (If you cut thicker pieces of meat, the grilling times can be extended a little.) Watch that the flames created by the dripping bacon fat don't burn the bits too badly. Remember to remove the toothpick before eating; sometimes the ends are burned off and you can't see them. These are great for appetizers or as a main course!

KEN BOWMAN
Apollo, Pennsylvania

ALFRED M. DENNIS
Newbury, Indiana

A. J.'S HONKER PÂTÉ

2 goose breasts, skinned and boned
4 pounds braunschweiger
1 pint mustard
1 pint salad dressing (Miracle
    Whip suggested)
¼ tablespoon salt
¼ tablespoon pepper
Garlic powder to taste

Preheat oven at 325°F. Bake the goose breasts until they are tender and juicy, about 1½–2 hours. (If they are small, cook some more breasts.) Remove and cool. Grind the breasts into a fine texture. Place the ground breast meat and braunschweiger in food processor. Add mustard, salad dressing, pepper, salt, and garlic powder. Process to desired consistency.

A. J. CHRISTIANSEN
Kimball, Nebraska

A. J.'S PÂTÉ BLOSSOMS

3–4 pounds fresh mushrooms,
    any variety with caps
2–3 pounds Honker Pâté
    (see previous recipe)

Take a large silver platter or a couple of paper plates. Cover surface with lettuce leaves. Clean mushrooms and remove the stems. Sauté whole mushroom caps in butter, open side up. Place mushrooms on top of the lettuce. Fill a pastry bag with the pâté and squeeze into mushroom caps. If you like, sprinkle a little paprika on top.

A. J. CHRISTIANSEN
Kimball, Nebraska

FISH SPREAD

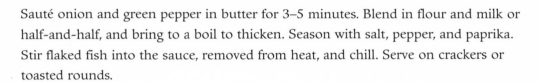

1 small onion, diced

1 small green pepper, diced

3 tablespoons butter

2 tablespoons flour

1 cup milk or half-and-half

Salt, pepper, and paprika to taste

1 cup cooked fish, such as salmon or northern pike, flaked (bones removed)

Sauté onion and green pepper in butter for 3–5 minutes. Blend in flour and milk or half-and-half, and bring to a boil to thicken. Season with salt, pepper, and paprika. Stir flaked fish into the sauce, removed from heat, and chill. Serve on crackers or toasted rounds.

JIM TROCHTA
Suring, Wisconsin

Peking Duck Hors d'Oeuvres

Cut boneless duck breasts crosswise into thin slices, then into bite-size pieces no bigger than ½ inch. Marinate in Yoshida's Original Gourmet Sauce for 2–4 hours, then drain and fry in olive oil. Do not overcook.

Dunk rice paper (8½-inch diameter) in near-boiling water until soft (approximately 5 seconds), turning as needed. Be careful not to burn your fingers!

Place rice paper on a plate and spoon on about a teaspoon of Chinese-style plum or duck sauce (apricot flavor). Place cooked duck on rice paper and add chopped green onions to taste.

Fold rice paper into a pocket and eat with fingers.

PAUL SADLER
Bellingham, Washington

MONTANA FISH COCKTAIL

½–1 cup finely diced celery

5–6 green onions, chopped

1 batch Cocktail Sauce (see page 197)

1 pound yellow perch, bass, or pike skinless fillets (or shrimp)

Combine celery, green onions, and Cocktail Sauce and chill. Cut fish into bite-size pieces, put into strainer, and poach in boiling water for 30 seconds. Remove and plunge into ice water to stop the cooking. Drain well. Mix into sauce and chill for 4–6 hours before serving.

TERRY LINDLEY
Bigfork, Montana

FRESH SALMON SPREAD

¾ pound fresh salmon fillet

3 12-ounce containers of cream cheese, softened

3 stalks celery, chopped

1 small onion, chopped

Boil salmon in a small amount of water until cooked through; let cool. Remove the skin from the salmon and flake salmon into small pieces. Combine the salmon with all other ingredients and mix thoroughly until well blended. Store in a tightly covered container and chill for 2 hours. Serve with crackers.

RON AND KAY DUNLAP
Onaluska, Washington

CHEESE DIP IN FRENCH BREAD

1 round French bread
1 bunch green onions, chopped
1 tablespoon butter
10 cloves garlic, minced
8 ounces cream cheese, softened
1 pint sour cream
12 ounces sharp cheddar cheese, grated
1 12-ounce can water-packed artichokes, chopped
1 6-ounce can water chestnuts, chopped

Slice off top of round bread (reserve top) and scoop out insides. Sauté green onions in butter. Combine with remaining ingredients and place in scooped-out bread round. Double-wrap stuffed bread (with top on) in aluminum foil and bake at 350°F for 1½ hours.

EDITH FERRARIO
Central Point, Oregon

SMOKED FISH SPREAD I

4 ounces smoked fish, skin and
    bones removed
1–2 tablespoons sour cream
1 3-ounce package cream cheese,
    softened
1 tablespoon parsley
Garlic powder to taste

Put fish in mixing bowl or food processor
with rest of ingredients. Blend until smooth.
Let chill for 2–3 hours. Serve with crackers
(a cold beer doesn't hurt, either).

TERRY LINDLEY
Big Fork, Montana

SMOKED FISH SPREAD II

1 pound smoked fish, skin and
    bones removed
½ pound cream cheese, softened
1–2 green onions, chopped
1 tablespoon lemon juice
½ teaspoon salt
⅛ teaspoon black pepper
1 teaspoon dill
1–2 tablespoons mayonnaise
1–2 tablespoons sour cream
1 tablespoon paprika
2 tablespoons capers

In mixing bowl or food processor, blend
until smooth all the ingredients except the
capers. Then stir in capers. Cover and let
chill for 2–3 hours. Serve with crackers.

TERRY LINDLEY
Big Fork, Montana

BEER-BATTERED, STUFFED, DEEP-FRIED MOREL MUSHROOMS

4 large (6-inch) fresh morels or 6–8 smaller ones

8 ounces cream cheese, softened

¼–½ cup chopped fresh chives

2 eggs, well beaten

⅔ cup beer

1 cup flour

½ teaspoon salt

2 tablespoons vegetable oil

Vegetable oil for deep-frying

2–3 cloves garlic, crushed

Clean and dry morels, then slice in half lengthwise. Combine cream cheese and chives. Stuff each morel half with cream cheese mixture. Fit halves of mushrooms back together. Refrigerate for 1–2 hours to harden cream cheese.

Make batter by combining eggs and beer, then slowly beating in flour, salt, and 2 tablespoons vegetable oil. The batter should be smooth. Heat oil in frying pan to 375°F (oil should be deep enough to submerge the morels). Add crushed garlic to oil and remove when garlic turns light brown. (This flavors the oil but keeps the garlic from burning and turning your oil brown.) Coat stuffed morels very well in batter to seal the cream cheese into the mushrooms. Deep-fry in hot oil until golden, about 10 minutes. Drain on paper towels. Serve hot as is, or with salsa, French onion sour cream dip, or horseradish sauce.

MARY ANNE LECCE
Collinsville, Illinois

A. J.'S STUFFED CELERY

1 3-ounce package cream cheese, softened
2 ounces blue cheese
4 tablespoons butter, softened
2 tablespoons finely chopped green pepper
2 teaspoons finely chopped onion
1 shot bourbon (optional)
4–6 celery stalks, cut into 3-inch chunks
Salt and paprika

Combine cream cheese, blue cheese, and butter. Add onion and green pepper. Stir in bourbon, adding enough to make the mixture spreadable. Stuff celery stalks with the mixture and sprinkle with paprika and salt.

A. J. CHRISTIANSEN
Kimball, Nebraska

Heather's Hot and Spicy Venison Soup

Thinly slice medium-size venison roast into fork-size pieces ⅛ inch thick. Place in large kettle or Crock-Pot and brown in small amount of oil, stirring constantly. Add 2 bouillon cubes, 1 pint canned tomatoes, 3 handfuls frozen corn (or 1 can corn, drained), 2 or 3 sliced potatoes, water to about 3 inches of top of Crock-Pot and creole seasoning to taste (approximately 2–3 tablespoons). Let simmer on low until potatoes are tender, about ½ hour. Serve with Italian bread and salad.

HEATHER HARROD
Kentucky

WILD GOOSE AND WILD RICE SOUP

8 ounces uncooked wild rice (about 1⅓ cups)

2 small wild geese, skinned

2 tablespoons butter

12 ounces mushrooms, sliced

1 cup chopped onion

1 cup chopped celery

2 tablespoons instant chicken bouillon granules

¾ teaspoon white pepper

Salt to taste

4 cups water

¾ cup dry white wine

Cook wild rice according to package directions, but cook only for 30 minutes. Drain off excess liquid and set rice aside.

In a 5- or 6-quart stock pot, combine the geese with 7 cups of water. Bring to a boil, then reduce heat and simmer (covered) for 1 hour (until meat is tender). Remove geese from broth and let stand until cool enough to handle. Skim fat from broth, then strain and reserve broth. Remove goose meat from bone and cut into bite-size pieces. Set aside.

In same pot, melt butter and cook mushrooms for 4–5 minutes (until tender). Add onion and celery. Cover and cook for 5–10 minutes (until tender). Return strained broth to pot and add the partially cooked wild rice. Stir in the bouillon granules, white pepper, and salt. Add 4 cups water. Bring to boil. Reduce heat and simmer, uncovered, for 15 minutes. Stir in goose meat and wine. Heat through and serve.

MARY ANNE LECCE
Collinsville, Illinois

MARY'S ELK GAZPACHO

**1–1½ pounds elk (loin or rump is best), cut into ½-inch cubes, trimmed of
  fat and fascia**

6 or more tablespoons olive oil

5–6 cloves garlic, minced

2 medium sweet onions, diced

2 cups water

Ice cubes

3–4 green peppers

1 large cucumber, sliced thin

3–4 medium tomatoes, cut in small pieces

1½ cups bay shrimp, cooked

4 slices cooked, processed ham, cut in pieces

1 package pepperoni, sliced thin

6 slices stale bread, broken into pieces

1 tablespoon crushed oregano

½–1 teaspoon salt

3 tablespoons garlic-flavored wine vinegar

Sauté elk cubes in 3 tablespoons olive oil on medium-high heat for 4–5 minutes. Add
more oil if necessary. Add garlic and onion and sauté for 2 more minutes, being careful not to burn the garlic. Add 2 cups water and let simmer on low until elk is tender
(1–2 hours). Add 10–12 ice cubes to cool broth quickly, and set aside.

   Over open flame or under broiler, blister green peppers until outer skin is black.
Place peppers in a paper bag and let sit for 15 minutes. Peel off skins, shred peppers
into small bits, and place in a large bowl. Add cucumber, tomatoes, shrimp, ham,

pepperoni, bread, oregano, ½ teaspoon salt, 3 tablespoons olive oil, and vinegar. Stir. Add elk chunks and garlic/onion broth and more water if desired to thin mixture, and stir again. Refrigerate in covered bowl. Serve in soup bowls, adding more salt, vinegar, and olive oil to taste. Best the second day. Serves 6.

THOMAS S. McCONNELL
Albuquerque, New Mexico

Chislic: A Cubed Meat Treat

There are numerous ways to enjoy the wild game we harvest, but nothing quite compares to preparing it in "chislic style."

It is not known for sure where the term "chislic" originated. Some geographical areas have never even heard the word, let alone enjoyed this true delicacy. In my area of south-central South Dakota, however, it is a very well known term.

As near as I can tell, chislic originally was goat meat, but most people I know use the term with any meat that is cubed and deep-fat fried. My favorite way to make it is to cube meat into ¾-inch squares, deep-fat fry it in oil, and season it with salt, garlic salt, Cajun spices, and/or onion-garlic powders.

It's best to remove all fat, membranes, and gristle. Pure meat is the best.

"Choice" meats are obviously the most desirable. Be sure the meat is well thawed and the cubes are not stuck together in clumps. Immerse into a 350°F bath of cooking oil. Allow the chislic to cook until it is a blackish-brown color. When it is nearly done, it will begin to float to the top of the oil. Remove the meat and drain it on paper to soak up the excess grease. Let the chislic cool a bit before eating. Five minutes or so on a paper towel should be sufficient. Then sprinkle it with the desired salts and spices.

The next time you invite your friends over to watch a ballgame, introduce them to chislic. Just be sure to have a good quantity of meat thawed and cubed; this stuff goes fast!

TOM MOYSIS
Brandon, South Dakota

ELK (DEER, MOOSE) HAMBURGER SOUP

1½ pounds ground deer, elk, or moose (or beef)

1 medium onion, chopped fine

1 teaspoon chopped garlic

1 tablespoon olive oil

1 28-ounce can tomatoes, chopped

2 cups water

3 10-ounce cans beef consommé, or 2 15-ounce cans beef broth

1 10-ounce can tomato soup

½ cup barley

4 large carrots, chopped

1 bay leaf

3 stalks celery, chopped

2 tablespoons chopped fresh (or dried) parsley

½ teaspoon dried thyme

Salt and pepper to taste

Brown meat, onions, and garlic in olive oil. Drain well. Combine with remaining ingredients in a large pot. Simmer, covered, for at least 2 hours (or all day), stirring occasionally to prevent sticking.

MARY ANNE LECCE
Collinsville, Illinois

VENISON VEGETABLE SOUP

1½–2 pounds venison, cubed

2 tablespoons olive oil

4 tablespoons sweet basil

5 tablespoons thyme

4 tablespoons oregano

3 quarts water

1 tablespoon peppercorns

3 bay leaves

2 tablespoons minced garlic

3 tablespoons seasoned salt

2 32-ounce cans diced tomatoes

1 16-ounce can tomato sauce

4 carrots, diced

3 turnips, peeled and cubed

2 rutabagas, peeled and cubed

1 large onion, diced

2 cups sliced celery

3 large potatoes, diced

Lightly brown meat in olive oil. Add 1 tablespoon each of sweet basil, thyme, and oregano. Cook until light brown. Then transfer to large pot. Add remaining ingredients. Bring to a boil, reduce heat, and simmer until meat is tender. Add more of listed seasonings to taste.

MICHAEL POOR
Yakima, Washington

CAJUN BLACK BEAN SOUP

1 pound dried black beans
1½ pounds smoked ham hocks
1½ quarts water
¼ cup dried minced onion
2 tablespoons paprika
½ teaspoon cayenne pepper
¼ cup minced green bell pepper
2 tablespoons chili powder
1 teaspoon salt
½ teaspoon ground cumin

In large kettle, combine beans, ham hocks, and water. Heat to boiling, then reduce heat and simmer, covered, for 2–2½ hours. Stir frequently and add more water if necessary to cover beans. To test for doneness, remove a few beans and taste. Remove ham hocks. Separate meat from bones, discarding fat and bones. Chop the meat and add back to soup. Stir in remaining ingredients, cover, and simmer for 1 hour. Remove ¾ of soup and puree in blender. Stir puree back into remaining beans. If necessary, add water to obtain desired thickness. Serve garnished with shredded cheese, sour cream, minced chives, or chopped eggs. Serves 8.

EDITH FERRARIO
Central Point, Oregon

The Last Word on Meat Care from the Rocky Mountain Elk Foundation

BY DON BURGESS

Many claims have been made and many books and articles have been written about right and wrong ways with meat. Despite the title of this chapter, there's really no such thing as "the last word" on the subject, and I doubt that there ever will be. Hunters—and especially *elk* hunters—are too innovative, too adventurous, and too rambunctious for that.

Take what you like from this piece, and do with it what you will. A lot of it's just my personal opinion on meat care, based on my own experiences with butchering, preserving, cooking, and eating whitetails, mule deer, antelope, and elk, all killed within 350 miles of my hometown.

For people with little experience or tradition in meat care, maybe this is a place to start. For people with lots of experience and different traditions, methods and opinions, it will provide some bones to pick. I only hope it leads to more enjoyment of what can and should be the healthiest, most delicious, most gratifying meat in the world: the wild game you've hunted, killed, butchered, and cooked for yourself, your family, and your friends.

A FEW OBSERVATIONS

Wild meat has been a staple food and primary source of protein for me and my family for at least four generations—on my father's side, anyway. I've eaten more wild game than I have beef, pork, and poultry. Forgive me, fellow elk hunters, but antelope is my favorite. Elk is tied with deer for second place. Mule deer and whitetail taste equally good to me. I like meat best—the top cuts, anyway—when it's cooked in a hot skillet on a grill, or over an open fire, flavored only with salt.

I've run into strong, repugnant gamy flavor with three or four animals I've killed in thirty-plus years of hunting big game: a three-and-a-half year-old mule deer buck killed in the heat of the rut; a buck antelope I killed many years ago under circumstances I don't recall now; and, just a few years ago, an older antelope buck whose back had been creased by another hunter's bullet a few days before I killed him. I'd watched that buck run a long time before he finally tried to run right up my rifle barrel.

I've killed a few animals that proved mild-flavored but tough. The young bull elk I killed shortly after the rut last year must have been chasing cows hard. He had little fat left on him, and the meat from even the choice cuts took quite a bit of chewing, even though I let him hang for two weeks at temperatures ranging from 25°F to 50°F before cutting and wrapping.

I had a number of bad experiences with meat from antelope my father killed when I was growing up. During those early October hunts out on the eastern Montana prairie, the daytime temperatures often reach into the 60s or 70s, and I don't believe Dad cooled down some of his antelope as quickly as he should have. For sure he never used the most effective cooling technique I know of, which is immersing the entire field-dressed carcass in the nearest cool waterhole until all the heat has gone out of it. But more on that later.

The rutting mule deer buck was the worst case. My wife, Jan, and I were living in the foothills of the Bearpaw Mountains in north-central Montana, which in winter is one of the coldest places in the continental United States. I killed that buck about 2 miles from the house, brought him back whole and hung him from an aspen tree in the backyard. Although he was not a fully mature animal, he was the biggest-bodied and biggest-antlered deer I've ever killed. And although it was mid-November and he and a doe were shacked up off by themselves in the peak of the rut, he still had some fat on him.

He froze solid overnight. I pried out his tenderloins the next day, thawed them, sliced them into inch-thick medallions, and laid them in a very hot cast-iron pan with butter and salt. Those beautiful cutlets quickly shrank to tough little rinds about a quarter of an inch thick, with a smell reminiscent of strong armpit B.O.

I left that carcass hanging frozen solid for three weeks, not knowing exactly what

I'd do with it if it ever did thaw out. With no warmer weather in sight, I finally took it down and hung it in a commercial meat locker. It took about a week to thaw, and I let it hang another three weeks in that cooler, not so much because I believed it would improve the meat any, but because I entertained some deluded hope that it would disappear and I'd never have to deal with it.

The owner of the plant finally reminded me it was still there. I brought it back home, skinned it, and cooked up a little backstrap, fully expecting to have to turn it all into salami or feed it to the dogs. But the whole carcass turned out to be as sweet and tender as any deer I've eaten. Before that experience, I aged my meat because that's what my dad always did. Since then, I've done it with real conviction that it's good for the meat.

(If you decide to age your meat, expect to see mold growing on exposed meat surfaces in a week or two. Wipe it off, or trim it off when you're ready to cut and wrap. My dad always wiped those surfaces down with vinegar before starting to butcher an aged carcass. I seldom bother to do that, as those dry surfaces are trimmed away anyway.)

Lots of animals are mild and tender to start with. I've enjoyed very good eating with elk meat that I stripped from the bones in the field and sent directly from backpack to freezer when I got it home. But natural enzymatic processes within the meat will make it milder and more tender over time, provided it doesn't get colder than 32°F or warmer than 45°F for very long. I prefer to hang the whole or quartered carcass of every animal I kill for two or three weeks before I cut and wrap it. But if it warms up, I get it into the freezer right away.

Thawing individual packages slowly in the refrigerator and letting them sit there and age a few days before cooking and eating them works almost as well as hanging the carcass. I often take packages of my already well-aged meat out of the freezer and let them thaw in the refrigerator, then unwrap the meat and let it shed more moisture—sometimes allowing it to age another three or four days in the process—with great results.

Generally speaking, yearling males (spike bull elk), females, and the young of the year are fatter and more tender and have a milder flavor than older males. Almost all bulls and bucks are in better condition going into the rut than coming out of it. Most animals are fatter going into winter than coming out of it. If you have your choice of animals from a large group, and the time to study them, or a long season in which to stalk numerous animals and be selective, you can often identify sleeker, fatter, "beefier" individuals. Sheen and evenness of the coat is an indication of general well-being. But even an average-looking animal is likely to be a fine-eating animal.

If big antlers are what you're mostly after, you take whatever meat you get from underneath that spectacular headgear and make the best of it. Big old bucks and bulls are often very good eating, and there's a lot more meat on them. But some battle-weary, sexually exhausted bulls and bucks have to be ground up to be chewable and mixed with a lot of spices to be palatable. Still, before you turn them into summer sausage with a flavor that all those spices can't quite cover, try aging the beasts for two to five weeks. Then cut off some choice pieces, fry them up in a little butter and salt, and see what you think.

THE FUNDAMENTALS

Here are a few generally agreed upon rules for ensuring better meat:
- Make quick, clean kills.
- Quickly reduce internal muscle temperature on a fresh-killed animal to 45°F or less.
- Keep the meat clean and cool.
- Age the meat.
- Take care to keep meat clean while cutting and wrapping.
- Wrap meat in airtight packages for freezing.
- Thaw frozen meat slowly and let it drain thoroughly before cooking.

There are many opinions, pro and con, about other techniques and conditions that affect the quality of meat, such as which classes of animals are best eating, which weapons are best to ensure a quick, clean kill, and whether it's better to skin an animal right away or leave the hide on while it ages. There is some complexity here.

Some of these concerns overlap. Decisions critical to meat quality are affected by circumstances such as weather, time, topography, a hunter's physical abilities, and many other variables. Sometimes you just wing it. But if you at least know the fundamentals, chances are you'll be able to put good meat on your table from almost any animal you kill, under almost any circumstances.

MAKE QUICK, CLEAN KILLS

Stalk carefully, shoot well, and drop the animal with one shot without it ever knowing you are there. That's the essence of exciting, skillful, and ethical hunting. It's also the best start you can have toward putting good meat on your table.

If you drop an animal with one or two quick shots, you will almost always be able to find it and get it field-dressed quickly. Standard field-dressing technique ensures complete bleed-out: Taking out the windpipe, esophagus, heart, lungs, and intestines severs all major blood vessels leading into and out of the body cavity. Most of the blood in the head, neck, back and legs drains out when you gut an animal, if it hasn't already poured out through major veins and arteries severed by the bullet or arrow. My father always flexed the dead animal's legs vigorously after gutting it, believing that it more thoroughly expels the blood from the meat, and I habitually do it, too.

Of course, you'll have more edible meat if your bullet or arrow doesn't pass through meatier parts of an animal. A shot straight through the ribs behind the shoulder is ideal. A bullet in the ear or the base of the skull ruins even less meat, but it's not a good, ethical shot choice for most people. Unless you're a really good shot and have proven it in extensive target practice, and unless you have a steady rest and a very clear shot you know absolutely that you can make, there's too much risk of inflicting a terrible wound and losing the animal. I know a few of you can safely take that kind of shot because you've practiced a lot and have good judgment and great physical coordination—more power to you. The rest of us had better stick with the heart-lung shots, where we can wiggle a little and still hit the kill zone.

Wherever your bullet or arrow strikes, you'll wind up with better meat if you thoroughly trim away all damaged and bloodshot tissue around the wound channel, very soon after field dressing. I have no proof—just lots of hearsay evidence—that bloodshot meat tastes bad, and that coagulated blood that's collected between individual muscles can taint otherwise pure meat anywhere in the vicinity. But it sure looks bad to me, and I'll keep on trimming and discarding all bloodshot tissue and leave experimentation with it to somebody else.

COOL MEAT QUICKLY (AND KEEP IT COOL)

Bears, lions, coyotes, and wolves are always happy to cadge some easy meat. But the biggest threat is not the biggest critter. Unless it's pretty cold out, and unless you do a lot of things right in the first few hours after you've killed an animal—or throw a big party for everybody in your camp and eat the animal on the spot—you'll lose the meat to the lowly bacterium and/or a swarm of flies and wasps, at which point you might as well walk away and let the bigger critters in on the feast, too.

Bacteria flourish in warm weather and warm flesh. But if you can bring the internal temperature of the meat down from 100°F to below 45°F within two or three hours and keep it there until it's ready to cut and wrap, you'll win the battle with the bugs. If you take longer to get it chilled at the outset, your chances of winding up with good meat start going downhill. You may not know you've lost the battle until you cook and serve some of the choicest meat from deep inside the big ham muscles or shoulders, or even from the precious backstraps. It may not look bad or smell bad, and you won't know it's tainted until you put it in your mouth.

Opening up the body cavity and getting the entrails out quickly removes a lot of stored heat and allows air circulation, which helps cool the meat—as long as the air temperature is lower than the live animal's body temperature. Rather than remove the innards, some hunters immediately cut off the quarters (skinned or not skinned) and backstraps, then peel away the hide and fillet all the meat from flank, ribs and neck (see "Waste Not," Ted Kerasote's piece on guts-in field dressing, on page 70).

Either way, once you've opened up the belly, sternum, and throat and removed the innards, or removed all the meat without removing the innards, if the temperature is much above freezing you need to get the meat into a cool, shady ravine, or the shade of a cliff, bush or tree, and prop or hang it off the ground at least a few inches to allow air to circulate and cool all its surfaces.

The best way I know of to cool meat quickly is to immerse it in cold water. Heat is transferred much faster by water than by air. If it's at all possible, immerse the entire, field-dressed carcass in the nearest stream or pond as soon as you can. With animals too big to move whole, break them down into quarters and pack them to the nearest water. Unless it's a stinking elk wallow, it's not going to hurt the meat at all to throw the whole works in and leave it there until it's reached water temperature. I've been doing this for years whenever I kill an animal on a warm day. It could be one reason I've wound up with so little bad meat.

TAKE THE HIDE OFF, OR LEAVE IT ON?

Some people prefer taking the hide off immediately after they've killed and field-dressed an animal. Others prefer to leave it on until they've aged the carcass and are ready to cut and wrap the meat. The decision to skin or not to skin definitely makes a difference in cooling meat quickly, keeping it cool and keeping it clean.

There are advantages and disadvantages either way. Slipping the hide off a still-warm carcass is about as tough as peeling a banana. Hides and connective tissues begin to stiffen and dry as soon as animals are down and field-dressed, and the longer you wait to skin them, the harder it will be. If you hang a skin-on carcass outdoors or in an unheated building and it freezes solid, you'll have a real job on your hands to get the hide off. I've grossed out my wife and kids a couple of times by carrying whole frozen deer carcasses into the house to thaw them out so I could skin them.

So quick skinning is easier. But the most common argument for taking the hide off immediately is that it helps the meat cool quickly. The skin and hide are terrific insulation, definitely slowing the cooling process, so if the weather's balmy and there's not much chance of bringing that deep meat temperature down to 45°F within a few hours with the hide on, you should take it off.

One of the drawbacks to removing the hide immediately is that the surface of the meat is then exposed to dirt. If you plan on dragging the carcass back to your camp or your horse, or your vehicle, you don't want to take the hide off until the dragging's done (unless you have a clean tarp or sled to drag it on). But sturdy cotton sacks will help keep skinned meat clean. Cheesecloth game bags aren't very effective at keeping dirt off the meat, and flies can deposit their eggs right through them. Heavier cotton cloth, including common pillowcases, will do. Lightweight canvas bags are better.

Another problem with skinning the fresh carcass is that the outer surface of the meat starts to dry and harden when the skin is removed. If you like to age your meat for two or three weeks before cutting and wrapping, you'll wind up with a hard, dry rind—a fairly significant amount of good meat—that needs to be trimmed. It's extra work, and a waste of meat.

If there's plenty of water nearby, the hide can be an asset in the cooling process instead of a liability. Soaking a hide eliminates the insulating qualities of the hair, and an unskinned carcass immersed in water will cool nearly as rapidly as a skinned carcass. When you drag a carcass or quarters back out of a stream, pond, or stock tank, the water immediately begins to evaporate from the soaked hide. Evaporation is a very effective cooling method, the basic principle behind the swamp cooler. The meat, once cooled, will stay cooler longer with the hide on.

Immersing a carcass also cleans away residue from the field-dressing process, including blood, digestive tract contents, dirt, and debris. If you've left the hide on, immersion washes away stinky mud, urine, and any other offensive material clinging to the hide, and it helps persuade ticks and lice to leave the premises.

If you can't find a waterhole in which to dip the carcass, bring water to it. Haul it from the nearest source, pour it on the hide, and rub it in with your hands. If the meat is in a cotton game bag, soak the fabric. While you're packing the carcass back to trailhead or camp, and it's starting to warm back up, find water and chill the meat again the first chance you get. Do the same thing while it's hanging in camp, waiting for the trip home.

If you're driving home with the meat across long stretches of hot, waterless country, keep as much air flowing around it as possible. If you have more than one carcass, or several quarters, keep them separated so air flows around them. When you stop at convenience stores and gas stations, find a faucet and hose the meat down with cold water. Rinse the body cavities and all exposed meat surfaces, as well as the hides. Turn the carcasses belly up and fill the body cavities with ice if possible.

EXTREME MEASURES

If there's not much chance you'll be able to get a carcass chilled quickly even with air circulating all around it, and you can't get the carcass to cool water or cool water to the carcass, one option is to slice the large muscles to the bone in a few places (make the cuts parallel to the long leg bones or shoulder blades—*with* the grain of the muscles, not across them) and spread the sides of those cuts apart with the cleanest sticks or stones available so that the deep muscle heat is released faster. However, those deep gashes create more exposed surface area, and more chances for dirt, airborne bacteria, and other contaminants to reach the meat. If you make those gashes, you'd better process the carcass (cut, wrap and freeze it, jerk it, turn it into sausage, or can it) as soon as possible.

If you kill an animal someplace where there's *no chance* that the meat temperature will drop to 45°F within a few hours—the temperatures both day and night never dip that low, there's no cold water nearby, and you can't get the meat to a cooler place soon enough—what you'd best do is dry that meat. Dry meat won't spoil nearly as fast as fresh, raw meat.

Skin the animal and fillet all of the meat into strips and slabs not much more than an inch thick. Hang those strips and slabs out in the fresh air and direct sunlight, over fence wire or rope strung between trees, or on big, flat rocks in the hot sun where they can dry quickly. Speed the process by hanging the meat over a wide, low fire. To avoid a turpentine taste, don't use pine wood in the fire. Make a drying rack with green saplings or branches set horizontally above the fire, or string stove wire between poles or trees.

If you've planned ahead for warm weather and brought twenty pounds or so of table salt with you, apply it liberally to your meat while it's drying. The meat will taste great and keep longer. (By the way, a thorough application of salt to the flesh side of a fresh hide helps keep it from rotting.)

It could take two people a full day of steady work to set up a drying frame, get a good fire going and keep it going, and strip and dry all the meat from an elk carcass. But it's better than watching the meat spoil, which is not only against the law but also a sad and reprehensible waste of a fine animal and a lot of superb meat. When you're done, you'll have reduced the weight of pure lean meat by about 60 percent— 150 pounds becomes about sixty pounds. A stout hunter could pack all the meat from an entire full-grown elk on his back in one trip if it's dried first. The total time and energy spent drying the meat might be less than it would take to pack the meat out wet. Strip it, dry it, sack it up, pack it out, put it in the freezer, and enjoy the long, cold winter with lots of primitive-style jerky. Or rehydrate the meat and use it in soups, stews, and chili.

CLEAN, CAREFUL CUTTING, WRAPPING, AND FREEZING

Hide on or hide off, those big chunks of crude protoplasm can look pretty intimidating, if not revolting. The very idea of carving them up with a knife can be daunting.

It helps if you're really hungry before you start. If you haven't already removed and eaten the tenderloins—the long muscles lying along the underside of the spine near the hind quarters—begin the butchering process by cutting them away from the backbone with a long thin blade, trimming away any dried tissue and cleaning them up. The best move now is to cut them into long strands like string cheese, or across the grain into chunks or medallions, or dice them into nuggets—or leave them whole—and fry them in a hot pan with butter or cooking oil and salt.

Eat, and be transformed. Return inspired to the carcass cutting area. Envision the shapely roasts and steaks in that dark mound of meat. Imagine the burgers, the meat loaves, the stir-fries, and the stews to come. Take up your knife and approach the task with your mouth watering. Go at it like Michelangelo entering a block of marble with hammer and chisel, eager to reveal the splendor that lies within.

Make it a social or family event. Line up help; set up an assembly line. Or do it alone, meditatively, or thrashing. Just figure out how you might best do it, and do it. Don't worry. Be happy. If your intent was to end up with large, classic, commercial-style roasts, and you wind up instead with a lot of odd, ragged pieces, never mind.

They'll serve up fine. Invent and perfect your own devices, techniques, and styles. Reduce your wild game carcasses into slabs, strips, cubes, cylinders, heck, pyramids, if you like. Turn them into mountains of hamburger or 200 feet of linked Polish sausages. It's all good.

Prepare a spacious, clean surface and lay out your equipment. Provide plenty of good light. Music might be a good option. Set out two or three sharp butcher knives and/or filleting knives. You'll soon figure out which ones work best for you, and that they all get dull after a while. You'll find ways to keep them sharp. A meat saw can be helpful for quartering a carcass, removing antlers, cutting off the head, and reducing stripped rib cage, neck, and backbone to soup bones and doggie treats. Of course, a meat saw is a necessity if you like bone-in chops, roasts, and steaks. I never leave the bone in anymore, after a few experiences with soured meat right around the bone in some round steaks from deer I'd killed and butchered. It could be that the meat, being deep in the thickest muscle mass on the animals, hadn't cooled quickly enough in the field and would have been bad with or without the bone, but I remain suspicious of the bone itself. The rest of the meat was good, and I haven't had that problem since I stopped leaving the bone in.

It's good to have a clean surface long and wide enough to hold a quarter of an elk. A sheet of ¾-inch plywood over two sawhorses will do. Tape clean sheets of freezer wrap or other clean butcher paper over the wood surface. Tape new sheets on top of old as they become sullied and torn. A pan of warm water and a roll of paper towels or several cotton dish towels will help keep fingers, knives, cutting surfaces, and meat clean.

A cold, relatively dry carcass (one that's been hanging for a week or two or three) is firmer and easier to cut up than a warm, fresh carcass. For the same reason, it's better to do your meat cutting in a chilly room than in a warm room. Take the carcass apart and work on one quarter at a time. Lift and pull on the legs and you'll see where the joints are and where you need to cut. You'll learn anatomy quickly enough and get better at it every time you do it.

The front legs aren't joined to the torso by anything but muscle and fascia, and they come off easily with a few strokes of a sharp knife between leg and ribs, while lifting the leg out and away from the ribs. The hindquarters are more difficult; the ball at the top of the upper leg bone is joined to the socket in the pelvis by strong ligaments, and the joint is surrounded by the heaviest muscles on the elk's body. By lifting and flexing a hind leg, as if making the elk "do the splits," you'll be able to see where the joint lies. It isn't far from the surface in the inner groin area. Once you've exposed the joint, pop it open by lifting the leg some more and cutting the ligaments around the edge of the joint. Then sever the big interior ligament between ball and socket with the point of your blade, and finish cutting muscle tissue all the way around it, as near as you can get to the very base of the rump and thigh muscles where they connect to the pelvis.

Some of the best meat on a carcass will be left clinging to the pelvis. Trim it carefully away. Get all of it. Take a break from the work and heat up that frying pan again, and cook those precious morsels the same way you cooked the tenderloins— hot and fast in a little oil. Salt is all the spice they need. When my kids and company know I'm cooking these, they gather around and spear the pieces right out of the pan with forks and eat them hot, on the spot. A panful doesn't last long. My mouth is watering as I write this.

Separate and cut away large muscles in the front and hindquarters. Trim off tapered ends and toss them in a big bowl or pan to be ground later into burger. You can also package some or all of those pieces as stew meat, if they're from neck or flank or lower leg, or for stir-fries or shish kebabs if they're from more tender regions. There's no need to add beef suet to venison burger, by the way, unless you prefer the flavor and texture of fattier burger. Ground venison holds together in the pan—even on the grill, if you're careful with it—and tastes fine all by itself.

Package larger blocks of muscle as roasts. You can always make steaks out of them later if you want to.

Deep down among the big muscles of each hindquarter lies a small mass of blood vessels, fat, and lymphatic tissue. It's probably fine and nutritious, but I don't like the looks of it, so I trim it out and throw it away. (None of our scraps and bones go anywhere but back to nature. Our dogs especially love sections of rib cage and backbone, chopped or sawn into manageable pieces and set aside to dry for midwinter treats.)

Double-wrap meat for the freezer to guard against air penetration and freezer burn. Use clear plastic wrap for the first layer and freezer paper for the second, or use two layers of freezer paper. Or two sealable plastic bags, squeezing all the air out before you close the bags. Or use a vacuum-packing machine that sucks out the air and seals the meat inside special plastic bags. Or any combinations/improvisations you can think of.

Here's hoping you enjoy plenty of good hunting in seasons to come, and wind up with lots of prime, sweet, tender, wild meat to show for it. May you find pleasure in the kitchen, at the barbecue, and around the campfire as you try out the recipes in this book.

For an excellent graphic demonstration of field dressing, skinning, quartering, boning, and caping an elk, watch longtime Wyoming outfitter and RMEF supporter Ron Dube go to work on a freshly killed bull. His video, "Big Game from Field to Freezer with Ron Dube," is available through the Elk Foundation merchandise department. Phone 1–800–CALL ELK, ext. 402.

Don Burgess has been the hunting editor of Bugle *magazine since 1997. Born and raised in Montana, he's been eating elk and other wild game all his life.*

BREADS
AND PANCAKES

SOURDOUGH STARTER I

3 cups water
1 tablespoon (or 1 packet) dry yeast
1 tablespoon sugar
3 cups white flour

Mix all ingredients in a perfectly clean, large glass or ceramic bowl. Never use metal or plastic. Cover with a perfectly clean dinner plate. Let sit at room temperature for 48 hours. Pour starter into a perfectly clean glass or ceramic crock. Using perfectly clean containers helps guard against the starter from going bad. Let crock sit at room temperature.

When you take out starter for a recipe, put back equal amounts of flour and water. For example, if you take out 1 cup starter, stir ½ cup water and ½ cup flour back into crock. NEVER put anything but flour and water into crock or the starter will go bad. If the starter develops a clear layer of liquid on top, just stir it back in. That is natural for starters to do that. Try to use the starter at least once a week. If you miss a week, take out 1 cup starter and stir ½ cup water and ½ cup flour back into the remaining starter. This will help it to last. If for some reason the starter goes bad, discard it and start over.

LAURA NELSON
Providence, Utah

SOURDOUGH STARTER II

2 cups flour
1 cup sugar
1 package yeast
Water

Mix the flour, sugar, and yeast with the water to a consistency of pancake batter. Store in a gallon-size crock or glass jar with a plate covering the top. The starter will be ready to use the next day.

The sourdough is best if used every day. Just store at room temperature. However, if you do not use it every day, it can be stored in the refrigerator to slow it down. Never mix anything into the sourdough starter but flour and water. The nights before you want to use the sourdough, mix in the flour and water. Mix it to a consistency of pancake batter. The next day pour the mix out of the crock into a bowl. Pour out all but about a cup, which will remain in the crock as your starter.

To your sourdough in the bowl you can add eggs, sugar, bacon grease, milk, a dash of salt—just experiment. For hotcakes, mix thinner than for biscuits. The only thing that you never need to add is yeast or baking powder, as the sourdough is yeast and flour. If your starter gets too rank just pour out and discard most of the starter, then freshen it up with flour and water.

TOM SANDERS
East Ely, Nevada

SOURDOUGH DOUGHNUTS

2 cups flour
½ cup sugar
½ teaspoon nutmeg
½ teaspoon salt
1 teaspoon baking powder
1 teaspoon cinnamon
½ teaspoon baking soda
½ cup active sourdough starter
2 tablespoons vegetable oil
⅓ cup buttermilk (or soured milk)
1 egg
Vegetable oil for deep-frying

Sift together dry ingredients, then stir in remaining ingredients to create a dough. Roll out about ½-inch thick. Cut out with doughnut cutter.

Heat oil in a deep fryer. Oil should be quite hot. Drop doughnuts and holes a few at a time into hot oil. Turn each once until golden brown. Remove from oil and drop into a paper bag containing about 1 cup of sugar mixed with 1 teaspoon cinnamon. Shake bag to coat doughnuts and holes, and cool on paper towels.

Sourdough breads are always best while warm, as they become more dense and firm as they cool.

CHARLIE PIRTLE
Las Cruces, New Mexico

FAVORITE SOURDOUGH PANCAKES

2 cups sourdough starter

1 can evaporated milk (about 1⅔ cups)

2 cups flour

2 eggs, beaten

¼ cup sugar

2 tablespoons vegetable oil

1 teaspoon salt

2 teaspoons baking soda dissolved in 2 tablespoons water

Milk to thin batter (if needed)

In a large bowl combine starter, evaporated milk, and flour. Cover with a dinner plate and let sit at room temperature for about 12 hours. To this mixture stir in remaining ingredients in the order shown. Cook on greased preheated griddle or frying pan. (When temperature is about right, a drop of water will dance across surface.) When pancake is full of bubbles and edges start to look dry, flip pancake. Flip only once. Do not stack; this ruins the light quality of the pancake. Serve hot with butter and syrup.

LAURA NELSON
Providence, Utah

GRANDMA JOSEPH'S SOURDOUGH ELK HUNTER PANCAKES

2 cups unsifted flour
2 cups milk
¼ cup sourdough starter
2 eggs
1 tablespoon sugar
¾ teaspoon salt
¼ cup vegetable oil
1½ teaspoons baking soda

The night before, mix flour and milk in a bowl with the starter. Cover the bowl with a plate and leave out at room temperature overnight. The next morning, mix well until it is worked down. Be sure to take out ¼ cup of starter to save for next time. Beat in eggs. Then add sugar, salt, and oil. Mix well. Then dissolve baking soda in just a little bit of water and add to mixture. Fry pancakes on an ungreased griddle.

KEVIN AND ANNETTE JOSEPH
Dolores, Colorado

SOURDOUGH PANCAKES/WAFFLES

2 cups sourdough starter
2 rounded tablespoons sugar
2 eggs
Dash salt
1 teaspoon baking soda

I like my starter to be fairly thick for waffles and pancakes, so I mix it that way the night before. Put the starter in a large bowl. Add sugar, eggs, and salt. Mix well. When your griddle or waffle iron is hot—and well greased—add baking soda to the starter mix and stir vigorously. The soda will activate the mix and it will aerate, foam, and grow. This is what makes these pancakes and waffles so light. Pour onto griddle or into waffle iron and cook to a golden color. Mashed bananas, blueberries, strawberries, or chopped pecans can be added to the mix after the baking soda is put in.

If you are making pancakes or waffles for a big crew, it is best to make new batches instead of doubling or tripling the recipe, because the soda's effervescence doesn't last long and the batter goes flat, which diminishes the quality of the finished product.

CHARLIE PIRTLE
Las Cruces, New Mexico

FAVORITE SOURDOUGH BISCUITS

1½ cup sourdough starter

1 can evaporated milk plus enough water to make 2 cups of liquid

2 cups flour

1½ cups flour

1 cup flour

1¼ teaspoons salt

2 tablespoons sugar

2 teaspoons baking powder

1 teaspoon baking soda

6 tablespoons butter, melted

Mix starter, evaporated milk, and 2 cups flour in a large glass or ceramic bowl. Never use metal or plastic. Cover with a dinner plate and let sit at room temperature for about 12 hours.

To roll dough, first spread 1½ cups flour onto the counter top or other work surface. In a small bowl combine 1 cup flour, salt, sugar, baking powder, and baking soda. Blend well, then combine with sourdough and mix thoroughly. Turn dough onto floured work surface and knead gently for 1 minute. Roll out to ½–¾-inch thickness. Pour melted butter into three 8-inch round pans and coat pans evenly. Cut biscuits with a 2½-inch biscuit cutter. Put biscuits in pan then flip them so that biscuits are buttered top and bottom. Biscuits should be touching each other—about eight or nine per pan, depending on the size of biscuits.

Put a 9-by-13-inch pan of hot water at the bottom of oven. Put the three pans of biscuits on the top rack. Do not cover. Close oven and let biscuits rise 1½ hours. Carefully remove biscuit pans and the pan of water from oven. Preheat oven to 375°F. Return biscuits to oven and bake for about 25 minutes, or until tops are golden brown and they are cooked through. Serve hot with butter and honey.

LAURA NELSON
Providence, Utah

HOMEMADE ROLLS

½ **cup vegetable shortening**
½ **cup sugar**
2 cups milk
1 package quick-rising yeast
3 tablespoons warm water
Flour
1 teaspoon salt
2 teaspoons baking powder

Heat shortening, sugar, and milk in a saucepan until shortening melts. (Do not let this mixture get hot.) Set aside and cool to lukewarm.

Dissolve yeast in warm water and pour into lukewarm shortening mixture. Stir in enough plain flour to make a dough the consistency of cake dough. Put in a warm place and let dough rise to twice its original size. Then add salt and baking powder and mix really well with your hand. Add more plain flour to make the dough the consistency of biscuit dough (but not stiff).

Put dough in a large bowl and store in the refrigerator until you're ready to make your rolls. When you cut rolls out, place the rolls on a buttered pan, then set aside and let rise for 1 hour. Bake at 350°F to 400°F until rolls are light golden brown.

RON AND KAY DUNLAP
Onalaska, Washington

PANSY'S ROLLS

2 cups warm water
2 packages yeast
½ cup sugar
¼ cup vegetable oil
1 egg, beaten
2 teaspoons salt
6 cups flour

Mix all ingredients well. Put in a buttered pan and set aside to raise by about double. (This takes an hour in warm room.) If you want to roll out to make six crescent rolls, use a little more flour, let rise again, then bake at 350°F for 30–35 minutes.

These also make good hamburger buns. Make a double batch and freeze some.

PANSY BOWEN
Missoula, Montana

HUSH PUPPIES

1 egg
¾ cup buttermilk
½ cup chopped white onion
½ cup chopped green onion
1 cup yellow cornmeal
1 cup flour
2 teaspoons baking powder
1 teaspoon salt
1 teaspoon pepper
Oil for deep-frying

Beat egg and milk well, then add all other ingredients and mix well. Drop by table-spoonfuls into deep fryer until hush puppies float to the top and are golden brown. Serve hot with butter.

RON AND KAY DUNLAP
Onalaska, Washington

FAVORITE CORN BREAD

2 eggs
¼ cup sugar
¼ cup vegetable oil
1 cup milk
1 teaspoon salt
1 tablespoon baking powder
1 cup plus 3 tablespoons cornmeal
1 cup flour

Grease an 8- or 9-inch square glass pan. Preheat oven to 375°F. Beat eggs. Blend in oil and milk. Add remaining dry ingredients. Stir until blended. Pour batter into pan. Bake for about 30 minutes, or until top is golden brown and center springs back lightly when touched. Serve hot with butter and honey.

LAURA NELSON
Providence, Utah

HOBO BREAD

2 cups raisins
2½ cups boiling water
4 teaspoons baking soda
1 cup sugar
1 cup brown sugar
4 cups flour
3 tablespoons vegetable oil
1 cup nuts, chopped

Soak raisins overnight in the boiling water mixed with the baking soda. The next morning add the remaining ingredients. Mix well. Pour into two standard loaf pans. Bake at 350°F for 1 hour.

PANSY BOWEN
Missoula, Montana

FAVORITE PUMPKIN BREAD

⅔ cup vegetable oil

2⅔ cups sugar

4 eggs

2 cups cooked pumpkin

½ cup milk

1 teaspoon vanilla

2 teaspoons baking soda

1 teaspoon baking powder

1 teaspoon salt

2 teaspoons ground cinnamon

1 teaspoon ground nutmeg

½ teaspoon ground ginger

½ teaspoon ground cloves

½ teaspoon allspice

3⅓ cups flour

Grease three medium-size (8½-by-4½-by-2½-inch) loaf pans. Preheat oven to 350°F. In large bowl beat oil, sugar, eggs, pumpkin, and milk until well mixed. Add remaining ingredients and blend well. Pour into pans. Bake about 45–50 minutes or until toothpick inserted in center comes out clean. Carefully remove loaves from pans and let cool on cooling racks.

LAURA NELSON
Providence, Utah

HUCKLEBERRY BREAD

4 cups huckleberries

4 eggs

1 cup vegetable oil

1 cup milk

3 cups flour

2 cups sugar

1 teaspoon baking soda

1 teaspoon salt

Preheat oven to 350°F. Grease and flour two 9-by-5-inch loaf pans. In medium bowl combine berries, eggs, oil, and milk. In another bowl combine flour, sugar, baking soda, and salt. Add berry mixture to dry mixture and stir just until blended. Pour into pans. Bake for 1 hour, or until toothpick inserted in center comes out clean.

For a fun idea, grease and flour assorted cans (such as vegetable or fruit cans) to bake bread. Fill approximately ¾ full. Check after 45 minutes. Monitor until done.

DIANA JENSEN
Post Falls, Idaho

BUNGALOW ZUCCHINI BREAD

3 eggs

2 cups sugar

1 cup vegetable oil

3 cups flour

2 cups peeled and
   grated zucchini

3 teaspoons vanilla

1 teaspoon salt

1 teaspoon baking soda

¼ teaspoon baking powder

3 teaspoons ground cinnamon

Mix all ingredients. Put in bread pan and bake for 1 hour at 325°F.

SANDRA WATTERS
Orcas Island, Washington

POTATO DOUGHNUTS (SPUDNUTS)

2 cups milk

1 cup sugar

½ cup shortening

1 teaspoon salt

1 cup mashed potatoes

3 eggs, beaten

1 teaspoon vanilla or lemon extract

2 packages yeast

½ cup warm water

8 cups flour

Vegetable oil for deep-frying

Combine milk, sugar, shortening, salt, mashed potatoes, beaten eggs, and vanilla or lemon extract. Dissolve yeast in ½ cup warm water and add to mixture. Mix in flour until spongy. Let rise. Mix down and roll out to ½ inch thick and cut into doughnuts. (I use a tuna can to cut doughnuts out and a smaller cutter for the center.) Let rise again. Cook doughnuts in hot oil. Glaze while warm (put in a plastic bag and shake) or roll in cinnamon and sugar.

GLAZE

2 cups powdered sugar

3 tablespoons margarine

¼ cup milk

Mix sugar, margarine, and milk into a smooth glaze. Dip doughnuts in glaze and drain on wire rack over a cookie sheet.

PANSY BOWEN
Missoula, Montana

BRAN MUFFINS

2 cups bran buds
2 cups boiling water
1 cup shortening
2 cups brown sugar
4 eggs
1 quart buttermilk
5 cups flour
5 teaspoons baking soda
4 cups all-bran

Mix bran buds into boiling water and let stand to soften. Cream shortening with brown sugar, then mix in remaining ingredients and softened bran buds. Makes about 1 gallon. Can be stored in refrigerator and used as needed. Bake muffins in greased muffin pan at 350°F for 25–30 minutes.

PANSY BOWEN
Missoula, Montana

POTATO PANCAKES

3 cups finely grated raw
    potatoes, peeled or
    unpeeled
2 tablespoons flour
2 eggs
1 teaspoon salt
Milk

Rinse grated potatoes and squeeze out excess moisture (I roll them up in a clean towel). Mix with flour, eggs, salt, and enough milk to make a medium batter. Stir well. Ladle onto a medium-hot griddle or frying pan with ample oil. These cook slowly, so give yourself ample time.

Serve with applesauce or apple butter. You can also add grated onions or chopped red, orange, or yellow bell pepper for a different flavor.

SALLY KEMPLE
Portland, Oregon

Trade Secrets: What Butchers Know about Elk Hunting

BY BEN LONG

This man knows your secrets.

You can fudge the details with your hunting partner. You can fib to your family and coworkers. You can even deceive yourself. But this man knows the facts. He knows your failings and weaknesses, as well as your victories and strengths. He knows just how skilled you are with a rifle and a knife. He has examined the physical evidence. He is up to his elbows in reality, the reality of meat, day in and day out.

This man is your butcher. The fellow with the white apron, the keen blade, and the practiced hand. His boning knife is something like a scalpel, and he is part pathologist, performing an amateur necropsy every time he cuts and wraps a game animal. His examination of the evidence, literally tons of it, gives him an honest, unwavering, sometimes unflattering view of elk hunting.

Listen to butchers. You may be surprised at what you learn.

Meet Lyle Happel, of Bozeman, Montana. His Clean-Cut Meats processes hundreds of elk every year, and nearly twice as many mule deer and pronghorn antelope. The first alpine bulls are delivered to his door in early September, starting a parade of proud elk hunters that lasts through the final late hunts of February.

One cannot butcher that many elk and listen to that many elk hunters without learning a thing or two about modern hunting. When the quarters hang on Happel's meat hooks and the hide is peeled off, the truth is revealed. Bullet holes don't lie.

If the hunter was skilled and careful, if he did his job well, the only shattered bones and bloodshot meat Happel finds will be where the bullet passed in and out of the rib cage, the neck, or the head. Happel's job will be easy.

"If the bullet goes behind the shoulder blade, it only ruins a little rib meat," Happel says. "Try to avoid hitting the shoulder blade, or hitting too far back. If it's a head shot, the carcass looks just like it would coming out of a slaughterhouse."

If, on the other hand, the animal died hard, or if the shooter was trigger-happy or sloppy, there will be ruined meat to trim and toss into the garbage bin. In those unfortunate cases, Happel sees ragged wounds around the animal's edges, with one clipping an artery or severing the spinal column to end the animal's life, or collectively doing sufficient damage to reduce the animal to possession.

Sometimes years pass before a poorly hit animal is brought to ground. Happel estimates that four in ten adult animals he butchers have healed-over scars.

"You see quite a few old wounds," Happel says. "It's not very pleasant." All the butchers I talked with reported finding old wounds on elk, left by errant bullets and arrows from previous seasons. Typical injuries include mended leg bones that had been broken by bullets and broadheads buried in shoulder blades. Others are even worse: long-festering rump wounds, for example, from hunters who launched "hail Mary" shots.

"There are some people who will put lead in the air, just because there's an animal out there," Happel says. "That's sad. Anytime you put a bullet in the loins or hindquarters, you're going to be ruining top-quality meat."

There is little a butcher can do to save the meat of a poorly killed elk, such as a gut-shot or leg-busted animal.

"The longer they are stressed, the worse it is for everybody," says Happel.

Paunch hits are bad because they contaminate the meat with digestive acids. Equally bad are rump shots, which may reflect on a hunter's greed for a trophy or his impatience for "success" overriding his concern for his prey.

As the old hunter's saw goes, the work starts when the shooting stops. Hunting season sends tons of high-quality meat to freezers all over the country. But the sad fact is, too much meat never makes it to the table.

"There's a lot of game meat that gets wasted," Happel says. "And that's too bad. The way I see it, it's better just to let the wolves have it than to toss it in the garbage."

Actually, even butcher scraps are rarely wasted. Bone scraps, gristle, and other tissue are generally sent to a rendering plant, where they are boiled down to a paste that can be used for a variety of products. One of those products is cosmetics, such as eye shadow and lipstick. Here's a thought that's worth a chuckle: This morning some fashion plate in Los Angeles or New York may have smeared the remnants of your last elk on her face.

In most states, it's a crime to waste game meat. Even if such waste is not a crime, it's a damn shame. "We try to educate our hunters, our customers, when they come in," says Happel. "And frankly, there's a lot of education that needs to be done out there. A lot of hunters are not doing all they can to protect their meat."

With a hint of sadness in his voice, Happel recalls one balmy opening weekend in southwestern Montana. Two men lucked into a pair of fine bulls and made quick, killing shots. They gutted the bulls, secured pack horses, and dragged their trophies off the mountain to a waiting Suburban. Probably protecting the carpet with a tarp, they pulled the animals inside and drove home, exhausted.

The next day, they drove the Suburban, elk still inside, to Happel's shop. But by then, both elk had soured.

"I had to tell these guys they had just wasted two bull elk," Happel recalls. "It just broke their hearts. These guys, sometimes they almost break down and cry over their own ignorance, over their own lack of education."

A couple of generations ago, more hunters grew up on farms and learned butchery as children. More hunters started young and graduated into elk hunting slowly, mastering small game, then moving up to deer before tackling elk.

Now, the allure of elk hunting draws people inexperienced with smaller game or with caring for meat of any description. Some have no concept of the work that follows the kill. They don't know what they're getting into, and they don't carry the right tools.

John Peterson of H & H Meats in Missoula, Montana, says elk hunters are often underequipped to handle an elk. They forget to carry meat bags, a block-and-tackle, adequate rope, and a meat saw. They may have a knife, but probably only one, and no way to sharpen it when it dulls.

Peterson recommends hunters keep five-gallon buckets in their vehicles to carry water for rinsing the quarters. Another handy tool is a pump-up weed spray canister (one that has never been used with chemical pesticides). Filled with clean water, such a sprayer can blast away hair, pine needles, and other debris before it dries to the meat.

I once saw a hunter pack a how-to article ripped from a magazine on his hunt. He had all the tools he needed, and he planned to follow the step-by-step instructions when he shot something. At least he showed concern. But tools and instructions are only one half of the picture. Knowledge and experience is the other. Butchering is like auto mechanics or welding—a specialized skill that takes some time to learn. The average elk hunter might have to care for an elk once every four or five seasons. That's not a lot of practice. And the longer it takes to field-dress and otherwise cool down and process an elk in the field, the longer the bacteria has to work, and the greater the risk of spoilage, particularly when the weather is hot.

By far the biggest problem noted by game meat processors is spoilage of meat due to improper care after the animal is killed. When the meat is warm enough—generally over 40°F—bacteria multiply. When they multiply too much, the meat spoils, smells bad, and makes you sick if you eat it. In worst cases, it turns green from the inside and one whiff will make you retch.

"Bacteria is present, at harmless levels, in all meat," says Gary Baysinger of Mountain Meats in Craig, Colorado. "When the meat is properly cooled, bacterial activity is kept in check."

The equation is simple: bacteria + heat + time = spoilage. Too often, meat cutters agree, hunters fail to appreciate that as soon as a shot is fired, the race is on. There are two main rules to field dressing elk: Get the meat cool and keep the meat clean.

The problem isn't just dirt, but all bacteria-carrying contaminants. A common mistake noted by butchers is the use of dirty knives. They tell stories of hunters who rinse their knife blades in elk wallows in the middle of field dressing, then continue cutting. Bacteria from the dirty water spread everywhere the knife cuts.

Heat is a formidable enemy. It comes from two sources: internal body heat and external ambient temperatures. The elk's stomach and intestines are loaded with bacteria, which help the animal digest forage. The mass of tissues and organs inside the body cavity are also hot, and if left in place will keep the whole carcass warm enough, even in very cold weather, to allow bacteria to spread and cause spoilage.

That's why it's imperative to remove the entrails, first and foremost.

"If you talk to meat cutters around the country, you will hear a lot of the same stories," says Mark Buckley, of Buckley's Lockers Inc., in Newberg, Oregon. "We get guys who shoot a deer in eastern Oregon, throw it on an extended bumper, and drive four or five hours to us. They haven't even gutted it. People like that shouldn't even be given a license.

"Actually, elk hunters seem to do better than deer hunters," says Buckley, who frequently butchers both Rocky Mountain and Roosevelt elk. "Elk hunters are better prepared. Most of them know they have a big job ahead of them."

Even when an elk's insides are removed, the danger of spoilage is far from over. Elk shot in cold weather and gutted quickly can still spoil. Elk are big, hot-blooded animals that maintain a high metabolism. Elk meat holds heat because of its bulk.

"Most people can field-dress them okay," Happel says, "but they just don't go far enough." The best bet, the butchers agree, is to quarter the elk and leave it hanging from a tree in a cool creek bottom until it can be packed to the butcher's cooler. If an elk can't be quartered, it should at least be cut in half lengthwise. Only when there's no option should elk be left whole.

Even when quartered, meat can "bone sour" where its bulk is greatest: in the shoulders and hips. "Bone sour" is butcher's jargon for when an animal spoils from the inside out. It tends to occur at those major joints. A wise hunter opens up those areas with a knife or saw, allowing body heat to escape. An elk's thick mane insulates the neck, so butchers urge hunters to open the body cavity clear to the elk's chin if the bull isn't a trophy to be mounted.

Many hunters prefer to bring their elk out whole, however. Other times, a hunter may not have time to quarter an elk immediately. If an elk is to be left whole, there are several ways to minimize the risk of spoilage. An intact elk can sour on the side that is insulated by the earth. To prevent that, roll small logs under the carcass, prop it up off the ground, and allow air to flow around it. Leaving an elk in the back of a pickup with a shell or topper on it, even overnight, is asking for trouble. If it must be done, leave the windows open for plenty of ventilation. If two or more big game carcasses are stacked in the back of a pickup truck, the animals on the bottom are insulated by the ones on top, boosting the odds of spoilage.

Curiously, butchers disagree on other common tricks practiced to protect elk meat. Some butchers recommend packing the gutted elk's body cavity with snow before leaving it overnight. The theory is, the snow acts like a bag of ice, chilling the meat. Another butcher says that's a mistake, insisting that the snow actually insulates the meat, trapping heat inside. A scientifically minded hunter could settle that argument with a thermometer and a couple of elk.

Another debate revolves around whether the hide should be left on the quarters or whole carcass, or if they should be skinned. Baysinger says the answer depends on the air temperature. If it's warm, peel off the skin and cover the meat with cheesecloth. If it's cold, the hide will help protect the meat and keep it clean.

Hunters afield in summer weather of late August and early September must act particularly fast if they make a kill. Under some conditions, responsible hunters must simply exercise restraint. If you're far from your vehicle and even farther from the nearest ice or meat locker, and it's hot, and even the nights are warm, and there's no stream nearby for quickly cooling and cleansing the meat, and no deep shade areas in which to hang it, the best choice is not to shoot.

"When it's so darn hot, hold back," Happel says. "If you can't take care of that animal, stay home. This is especially true for early season bow hunters."

Another mistake that can lead to ruined meat in any kind of weather, if the meat has not cooled all the way through, is to wrap it in plastic garbage sacks or tarps instead of a porous, cotton cloth such as cheesecloth. Plastic traps air and heat, leading to soured meat. And cold weather alone is no guarantee of proper cooling. Indeed, if the cold air isn't circulating with relative freedom all around and through a carcass, bacteria may be growing and causing spoilage deep inside the meat even when the outside has begun to freeze solid.

A certain amount of meat is wasted each season because hunters don't know what to do with an animal that's tough or gamy. Some hunters are less than thorough when bringing home and cutting up the carcasses of older male animals in particular.

Common folk wisdom among hunters is that old, trophy bulls are tough and gamy compared with younger cows and calves. That's an oversimplification, many butchers say.

"I believe the quality of the meat has more to do with the kill and the care than it does the age of the animal," says Peterson. "Even if you've got an old bull, go ahead and make steaks and roasts out of it. Elk meat is so good, you don't want to make any assumptions until you're ready to put it on the platter. You can always grind it up to sausage or burger later if it proves to be tough."

Aging the meat can greatly improve tenderness and taste, and is worth trying, particularly if you cook up some of the freshly killed animal and find it tough. Ask your butcher if he has enough cooler space to leave an elk hanging before it's cut and wrapped.

In spite of all the mistakes and missteps that can be made, most hunters do make clean kills and return home with nutritious and tasty meat. It's a big job, and one that most hunters take seriously. It has been that way for a long time.

In his classic work, *Make Prayers to the Raven,* anthropologist Richard K. Nelson writes of Native American hunters in Alaska, who strive to not insult the spirit of the animal they rely upon for survival. Certainly, a hunter can commit no greater insult than to waste the meat of an animal, a gift given with its very life. And the best way to honor the animal is to enjoy every morsel of it.

Local meat cutters are happy to help you do just that.

Ben Long, a freelance writer based in Kalispell, Montana, was raised—and continues to thrive —on prime wild venison.

Field Dressing Step-by-Step

BY DAVID STALLING

Hunters sometimes haggle over whether it's best to gut an elk from front to back, or from back to front. No matter—as long as you remove the entrails as quickly as possible without puncturing them, and without getting hair and body fluids on the meat. Here's a common straightforward approach:

1. Roll the elk on its back, tying the legs out of the way with a cord or rope.

2. With your knife, make an incision through the elk's hide near the anus.

3. Lifting with the knife in one hand, while using the other hand to push the intestines and stomach out of the way, cut through the hide all the way up to the breast bone. *Do not puncture the internal organs.* Cut around the sex organs. In many states, sex organs must be left attached to the carcass.

4. Hold the entrails down with one hand, and, keeping your knife along the rib cage, cut the diaphragm—a membrane separating the lung and heart area from the stomach, paunch, and intestines. The diaphragm attaches the internal organs to the rib cage and needs to be cut so the entrails can be removed.

5. Cut through the hide above the breast bone and continue cutting up the neck to the chin. (If you plan to preserve a lifelike trophy mount, stop cutting the hide before you reach the brisket. The cape should be removed whole, peeled forward from a circular cut around the elk's torso, just behind the withers, down the sides of the front quarters to the breastbone a few inches back from the brisket. In other words, do not slit the neckhide from brisket to chin.)

Some hunters use a saw or hatchet to split the breast bone and open the carcass up even more. Cut the windpipe and esophagus at the upper neck and tie them off with cord. An elk's windpipe and esophagus sour quickly and will taint meat if not removed.

6. Keeping your knife close to the pelvic bone, cut a circle around the anus and tie off the intestines, keeping excrement from spilling on the meat. Some folks use a saw or hatchet to cut through the pelvic bone and open the animal up even more.

7. Reach up into the chest cavity and grab the windpipe and esophagus. Carefully work loose the internal organs and slide them out of the animal. It helps to have the rear of the animal facing downhill. If you like the heart and liver, cut them out before you slide the entrails into the dirt. Put them in a small bag to keep them clean and out of reach of birds and insects.

8. Drain the body cavity, clean it, dry it with a towel, and prop it open with a stick. Some hunters leave their elk at this stage to return later with help. But the carcass cools faster if you bone or quarter it right away.

An avid bowhunter, backpacker, and wildlands advocate, David Stalling worked ten years for the Rocky Mountain Elk Foundation as the conservation editor for Bugle *magazine. He now works for Trout Unlimited. He and his wife, Christine, and son, Cory, live in Missoula, Montana.*

SIDE DISHES

CALICO BEANS

1 can butter beans
1 can lima beans
1 can red kidney beans
1 can pork and beans
1 pound ground beef
¾ pound bacon
½ cup dark brown sugar
½ cup ketchup
Molasses to taste
Dash salt and garlic salt

Drain liquid from butter and lima beans. Put all beans and liquid from kidney beans and pork and beans in a beanpot or baking dish.

In a frying pan brown the ground meat and bacon. Drain off all fat. Add the cooked meat and all remaining ingredients to the beans. Bake at 350°F for 1 hour or in an electric Crock-Pot on high for 5 hours.

EDITH FERRARIO
Central Point, Oregon

CHILES RELLENOS

2 10-ounce cans whole chiles

¾ pound Muenster cheese, shredded

3 tablespoons flour

1 tablespoon water

¼ teaspoon salt

1 cup vegetable oil

3 eggs, separated

Stuff chiles with cheese and set aside. In a medium bowl beat egg whites until peaks form. In another bowl beat yolks, water, flour, and salt. Fold egg whites into yolk mixture. Dip chiles one at a time in this mixture and fry in oil. Cook on both sides. Lay on paper towels to drain. Remove from paper towels and place on plates. Top with tomato sauce.

TOMATO SAUCE

1 tablespoon vegetable oil

½ cup chopped onion

2 cloves garlic, minced

4 large tomatoes, peeled and
chopped (or 1 28-ounce can
of tomatoes)

10 peppercorns

9 whole cloves

2 cinnamon sticks or a little
cinnamon oil

½ teaspoon salt

¼ teaspoon thyme

¼ cup red wine

¼ cup sugar

Heat oil. Add onion and garlic and sauté until tender. Add remaining ingredients and simmer uncovered for 15 minutes (while you fry rellenos).

CAROL ALEXANDER
Montrose, Colorado

ROSARIO'S MEXICAN RICE

1 cup rice
1 tablespoon oil
1 onion, chopped
1 tomato, chopped
1 teaspoon cumin
1 teaspoon oregano
Salt
2 cups water
1 tablespoon tomato paste

Brown rice in oil, add onions and tomato, and cook until onion is translucent, stirring often. Add cumin, oregano, salt, water, and tomato paste. Cover and simmer about 20 minutes.

CAROL ALEXANDER
Montrose, Colorado

BROCCOLI AND CRANBERRY SALAD

1 cup mayonnaise
⅓ cup sugar
4 tablespoons vinegar
4 cups chopped broccoli florets
10 slices bacon, cooked crisp and
    crumbled
½ cup minced onions
1 cup cranberries
1 cup shredded mild cheddar
    cheese

Mix mayonnaise, sugar, and vinegar together. Pour over other ingredients. Toss to combine. Refrigerate for 1½–2 hours. Serves 8.

SUZETTE HORTON
Idaho Falls, Idaho

POLENTA

3 cups chicken bouillon

1 cup polenta

Chopped green onion to taste

Chopped parsley to taste

1–1½ cups Monterey Jack, Swiss, and/or blue cheese

Parmesan cheese

Bring bouillon to a boil, remove from heat, and add polenta all at once, stirring with a whisk so there will be no lumps. Return to burner and continue to stir until it comes to a slow boil and starts to thicken. Cook over low heat for about 45 minutes, stirring every once in a while so it doesn't stick to the bottom of the pan. Add more bouillon as needed. Just before serving, stir in green onions, parsley, one or more of the cheeses (use at least a cup of cheese), and a small amount of Parmesan. Serves 4.

EDITH FERRARIO
Central Point, Oregon

Cowboy Beans

Cut 2–3 strips of bacon in pieces. Put in frying pan. Chop 1 small onion or 2–3 green onions and add to bacon. Cook until brown. Add 2 15-ounce cans pork and beans, ⅓–½ cup ketchup, 1 cup brown sugar (more or less to your taste), and ½ teaspoon dry mustard.

Variation #1: Fry hamburger with bacon and onion. Draw off grease.

Variation #2: Add chopped wieners.

PANSY BOWEN
Missoula, Montana

EGG PUFF

10 eggs
½ cup flour
1 teaspoon baking powder
½ teaspoon salt
1 pound Monterey Jack cheese
½ cup melted butter
1 pint small-curd cottage cheese
1 4-ounce can green chiles

Beat eggs until lemon in color. Mix remaining ingredients and add to the egg mixture. Butter a 9-by-13-inch casserole dish and pour in the egg mixture. Bake at 350°F for 30–40 minutes.

RON AND KAY DUNLAP
Onalaska, Washington

Shortcut Cole Slaw

The name refers not to how you cut the cabbage, but to a preparation shortcut, timewise.

Shred cabbage, onion, and bell pepper. Season with salt, pepper, and garlic salt. Add ranch dressing until slaw is creamy enough to suit you. Ready to serve. Small, whole ripe olives make a nice addition to this side dish.

CHARLIE PIRTLE
Las Cruces, New Mexico

CORN CASSEROLE

1 small onion, diced

½ cup margarine

1 15½-ounce can whole kernel corn, undrained

1 15½-ounce can cream-style corn

1 box Jiffy corn muffin mix

3 eggs, beaten

½ cup sugar

Salt and pepper to taste

½ pint sour cream

1½ cups grated cheddar cheese

Sauté onion in margarine. Add both cans of corn, muffin mix, eggs, sugar, salt, and pepper. Mix well. Stir in sour cream and cheese. Pour into greased 9-by-13-inch pan or a Dutch oven. Bake at 350°F for about 1 hour, until brown and crusty.

PHYLLIS FUNKHOUSER
Paris, Illinois

FRIED GREEN TOMATOES

4–6 medium green tomatoes
1 egg
3 tablespoons milk
Salt and pepper to taste
⅔ cup Italian seasoned bread crumbs
2 tablespoons Parmesan cheese
Oil for frying
2–3 cloves garlic, crushed
2 tablespoons butter

Slice tomatoes horizontally in ½-inch slices. Mix egg, milk, salt, and pepper in a shallow bowl. Combine bread crumbs and Parmesan cheese in another shallow bowl.

Add oil to skillet to a depth of about ¼ inch and heat oil. Add crushed garlic cloves, but remove them when they turn light brown before frying tomatoes. (This flavors the oil but keeps the garlic from burning and turning your oil brown.)

Dip tomato slices in the bread crumb mixture, then the egg mixture, and then again in the bread crumb mixture to coat well. Add butter to skillet and heat until melted. Cook tomatoes over medium heat, turning, until light brown. Drain on paper towels. Serve hot.

MARY ANNE LECCE
Collinsville, Illinois

MINCEMEAT SALAD

1 3-ounce package orange gelatin

1 cup hot water

¾ cup orange juice

1 cup prepared mincemeat

1 cup nuts

Dissolve gelatin in water. Add remaining ingredients. Pour into a lightly greased 1-quart mold and chill until set. Serves 8.

CAROL ALEXANDER
Montrose, Colorado

REAL Garlic Mashed Potatoes

Boil 12 large red potatoes with the skins on (or 8 regular potatoes) in a large pot with 7 large cloves of chopped garlic.

After potatoes have cooked, remove pot from heat, add 3 cloves of crushed garlic to the water, and let stand for 10 minutes. Then drain, while leaving all of the crushed garlic with the potatoes.

Crush potatoes with a large fork or spoon. Now mash or beat potatoes while adding to the potatoes ⅓ to ½ cup of heated milk, ⅔ stick of butter (melted or softened), 3 tablespoons olive oil, 2 tablespoons sour cream, 3 cloves of thoroughly crushed or finely chopped (or pureed) garlic, and 4 teaspoons of chopped fresh parsley.

Garnish with large sprigs of fresh garlic shoots. You did say you liked garlic, didn't you?

JAMES PINCH
Spokane, Washington

Waste Not

BY TED KERASOTE

The carcass lying in the snow told the story. The elk had been shot on the hillside above, dragged down to the creek, gutted, and skinned. The rear end of the animal had been separated from the spine forward of the hips, and, if the imprints in the snow and the piles of bone dust could be trusted, the pelvic girdle had been sawed in half, creating two hind quarters. The front shoulders and backstraps had been taken off, leaving behind the rib cage, neck, and head of the cow elk, plus the four lower legs, which had been sawed off their respective limbs at the knees. A fairly neat job.

However, as I stood and looked at the carcass, I could see that it still contained valuable meat: An easy 30 pounds of potential burger and sausage remained on the ribs and neck. Why hadn't it been taken?

More than likely the hunter had expended time and energy gutting, skinning, and quartering the animal, and when it came time to bone out the ribs and neck, he or she found the day waning, the several heavily laden round trips to the canyon rim daunting, and the prospect of returning in the dark or the next day unappealing. The meat on the front part of the elk was left behind.

The story is repeated wherever hunters kill elk far from the road; weariness frequently prevails over good intentions. However, there is an alternative way to field-dress and dismember an elk that does not involve eviscerating and sawing an animal into quarters. Called filleting, it saves time and energy that can be better applied to boning out all the edible muscle meat. By leaving the greater portion of an elk's skeleton in the field, it also allows the nutrients contained in its bones to return to the ground where the animal lived rather than storing them uselessly in a landfill far away.

This clever method of field dressing was shown to me by game processor Terry Swart of Belgrade, Montana. Having tried filleting, I would never go back to the gut-and-saw procedure.

For most of us there is no compelling reason to eviscerate an animal, since few of us eat intestines or lungs or use the stomach for containers. Instead, consider elk meat as fruit with a pit deep inside: Instead of taking out the pit, you peel away the fruit and leave the pit behind. (If you want to eat the organ meats like heart, liver, and kidneys, just retrieve them at the end of the filleting process.)

1. The first step in the filleting process is to skin the elk. This can be done on the ground by skinning one side, then rolling the elk over and skinning the other side, either before or after you've removed the meat from the first side. Skinning helps cool the carcass and provides a tarp on which to lay boned-out meat, keeping it clean. Tanned with the hair off, the hide also gives you valuable leather for clothing, or, tanned with the hair on, a bedspread, couch covering, or wall hanging. If you don't want the hide, the following steps can be done without completely removing the hide from the elk.

2. Take off the four lower limbs by working your knife into the knee joints. This eliminates the need for laborious sawing. On the rear legs try not to cut through the Achilles tendons so as to retain these convenient handles for carrying or hanging.

3. Taking off the front shoulder by pulling it away from the rib cage and cutting into the armpit and around the scapula. Place the front shoulder in the snow, on the flesh side of the hide, or in a game bag. Hang it in a tree if possible. If it's cold, game bags keep meat clean as it is put in packs or panniers and then loaded into vehicles. If it's warm, game bags also keep flies from laying their eggs in the meat. Hanging the meat allows air to circulate and cool the meat uniformly.

4. Remove the backstrap from neck to hip. The backstrap is the long piece of muscle that sits along the vertebrae.

5. Remove the hindquarter by boning it out from the pelvic girdle and cutting the tendon at the ball-and-socket joint. Hang the hindquarter or place it aside.

6. Beginning at the sternum, bone out the meat that covers the ribs. Continue all the way to the spine. Then bone out the entire neck all the way to the ears and chin. Go back and remove the strips of meat that lie between the ribs. Trim away blood-shot meat and damaged tissue around the bullet or arrow hole.

7. Push the viscera away from the backbone between the last rib and the pelvis and remove the tenderloin, the long strip of meat that lies next to the backbone on the interior of the animal.

8. Roll the elk over and repeat steps three to seven on the other side of the animal.

9. If you want the edible organs, remove them from the abdominal and thoracic cavities, which are now easily accessible.

Before you now lies the almost-complete skeleton of the elk, devoid of any muscle meat except what's left on the head, which, if you're diligent, you can skin and bone out as well. Not only have you saved considerable time by not gutting the animal or sawing through pelvis, spine, ribs, and extremities, you have lightened your (or your pack animal's) loads by leaving bone in the mountains. On one 342-pound field-dressed cow elk, for example, the bones of the rib cage, spine, and pelvis weighed forty-two pounds and the four lower legs a total of twelve pounds. These could all be left behind.

Soon your four quarters are hanging in the trees, or in a cool shady place on the ground, on racks of poles or rocks to allow airflow underneath the meat. You can come back for them with a frame pack or with pack animals. Of course, you can also bone out these quarters, leaving the entire skeleton of the elk in the hills. However, the short lengths of bone in the quarters provide structure for handling and hanging this meat, if you wish to do the latter. Keeping the forequarter and hindquarter meat on the bone also keeps more of the meat from being exposed to the air until you're ready to butcher. Shrinkage is prevented; you get juicier steaks. (As an aside, many hunters over-age elk, losing valuable pounds of surface meat through drying. Tender cuts like backstraps, tenderloins, and hindquarter steaks, especially from young animals, can be eaten or frozen as soon as you get home.)

No matter which course you choose, place the boned-out meat in plastic trash bags (provided the meat is fully cooled to 45°F or colder before sacking it) and carry out a full pack of meat, especially the backstraps and tenderloins, from the kill site. If the site is visited and the meat scavenged in your absence by grizzlies, wolves, coyotes, ravens, or eagles, you will have at least preserved thirty or forty pounds of the best meat for your own consumption.

The average stiff hunting knife is not the best tool for filleting because it won't flex around the curvature of vertebrae and pelvis. I use two knives: a moderately stiff boning knife (a Victorinox Forschner 805-6) for skinning and for taking off the lower legs and forequarters, and a more flexible knife (a Victorinox Forschner 806F-6) for removing backstraps, tenderloins, and hindquarters. I've done an entire elk without resharpening either blade, which saves carrying a stone.

I must confess before closing that there is one major problem with filleting: Your hands stay so clean and your clothes so unbloodied that when you return from hunting no one believes that you've gotten your elk.

Ted Kerasote, veteran carnivore, RMEF Habitat Partner, and frequent contributor to Bugle, *also writes for many other magazines, including* Audubon *and* Outside. *He is the author of several books, including* Bloodties *and* Heart of Home. *He lives in Wyoming.*

ELK AND
OTHER MEATS

ROLLED STUFFED ELK ROAST

6 slices bacon

1 medium onion, chopped

½ cup chopped celery

½ cup chopped carrots

⅓ cup seasoned dry bread crumbs

2 teaspoons dried parsley flakes

¼ teaspoon salt

⅛ teaspoon pepper

3–4-pound elk roast (use a top or bottom round roast, no more than 1 inch
thick; butterfly if necessary)

3 slices bacon, cut in half

Fry 6 slices bacon in large skillet over medium heat until crisp. Remove from heat. Transfer bacon to paper towels to drain. Reserve 3 tablespoons bacon fat. Crumble drained bacon and set aside. Heat oven to 325°F. Sauté onions, celery, and carrots in reserved bacon fat over medium heat until tender. Remove from heat. Stir in crumbled bacon, bread crumbs, parsley flakes, salt, and pepper. Spread mixture evenly on roast and pat it firmly into place. Roll the roast up jelly-roll style, rolling with the grain of the meat. Tie roast with kitchen string. Place in roasting pan. Top roast with remaining bacon. Roast to desired doneness, 22 to 30 minutes per pound. Serves 6 to 8.

VICKIE HOPP
Bend, Oregon

ELK OR VENISON ROAST

¼ cup cider vinegar

¼ cup ketchup

5 tablespoons flour

1 teaspoon Worcestershire sauce

1 teaspoon dry mustard

½ teaspoon chili powder

2 teaspoons salt

¼ teaspoon pepper

2 tablespoons brown sugar or honey

5–6-pound elk or venison roast

4 strips bacon

1 stick (½ cup) butter

2 cups hot water

Combine first nine ingredients, blending until smooth. Spread spice mixture over meat and rub into it thoroughly. Put meat in roasting pan with bacon strips on top and fasten with toothpicks. Dot meat with butter. Pour 2 cups hot water around, not over meat. Roast uncovered at 450°F for 30 minutes, or until browned. Sprinkle with additional flour as spice mixture melts off (moisten flour).

Reduce oven to 325°F, cover roast, and continue baking for 3–4 hours until done and tender. Baste occasionally with drippings. Add more water if needed.

DWEE MURRAY
Oakville, Washington

VENISON LOIN WITH WHITE CREAM SAUCE

1 or 2 whole venison backstraps (it will still work if the steak is butterflied)

2 tablespoons freshly ground pepper

3 tablespoons seasoned salt

4 cloves garlic, chopped in big pieces

1 cup olive oil

WHITE CREAM SAUCE

1 stick (½ cup) butter

2 cups fresh mushrooms, sliced

1 stalk celery, diced

5 green onions, chopped

¼ cup flour

1 cup chicken broth

½ cup white wine

1 pint heavy cream

3 tablespoons Dijon mustard

Prepare sauce first. Melt butter in frying pan and sauté mushrooms, celery, and onion. Lower heat. Add all other ingredients and constantly stir until sauce is thickened and smooth. Set aside.

Get your grill smokin' hot! Thoroughly coat the meat with pepper and seasoned salt and cut small slits in the meat. Insert pieces of garlic in the slits. Coat the meat with olive oil and head to the grill. Sear the outside of the loin on both sides. Do not overcook. The meat should be medium rare. After grilling, slice the loin and pour sauce on top to serve. This is unbelievably good! Keeping the backstrap whole ensures the meat will be juicy.

JIM WEBER
Helena, Montana

ITALIAN CROCK-POT ROAST

3–4 pounds venison rump roast

1 8-ounce can tomato sauce

1½ cups water

1 teaspoon salt

1 teaspoon pepper

1 teaspoon dried parsley flakes

1 teaspoon garlic powder

1 teaspoon dried basil

1 teaspoon dried oregano

Dash Worcestershire sauce

Dash soy sauce

1 package Italian salad dressing mix

Put roast in Crock-Pot. Combine remaining ingredients in saucepan and cook over medium heat until mixture comes to a full boil. Remove from heat and pour over roast in Crock-Pot. Cook on low overnight or for 6–8 hours, on high. About 1½ hours before serving, flake meat apart and continue cooking. Serves 6 to 8.

NORM AND GAIL BRUCE
Minitonas, Manitoba

PHANTOM CREEK POT ROAST

1 pound elk roast
½ cup flour
2 teaspoons vegetable oil
½ cup soy sauce
½ cup red wine
½ cup water
½ cup chopped celery
½ cup chopped onion
2–3 cloves garlic, chopped

Coat meat with flour. Brown slowly in hot oil in Dutch oven or large skillet. Combine soy sauce, wine, and water. Add to meat with celery, onion, and garlic. Cover and simmer for about 3 hours, or until meat is tender. To make gravy, mix remaining flour with enough water to make a smooth paste. Remove meat and thicken slowly. To make this recipe in a Crock-Pot place all ingredients in pot and set it on low for 8 hours or so. Serves 4 to 6.

LESLIE COLLAR
Bailey, Colorado

CROCK-POT ROAST

2–4-pound deer or elk roast

1 medium onion, diced

1 apple, peeled and cored

3–4 cloves garlic

2 beef bouillon cubes

1 cup water

Cornstarch

Put onions, apple, garlic cloves, and bouillon cubes in Crock-Pot with water. Stir, then add roast. Cook on low heat all day or medium heat for about 5 hours or until done. Remove roast. Pour rest of ingredients into a blender to puree for gravy, using cornstarch as per directions on box for thickening. Serve with mashed potatoes and fresh bread. The apple really does it for the gravy!

GARY QUENZER
Cut Bank, Montana

CHUCKWAGON STEAKS

½ cup soy sauce

¼ cup beef consommé

1 clove garlic, crushed

1 tablespoon sugar

½ cup vegetable oil

Salt and pepper to taste

8 elk minute steaks,
    ¼–½ pound each

2 large onions, sliced

Mix soy sauce, consommé, garlic, sugar, oil, salt and pepper in a 9-by-13-inch pan. Add steaks and marinate, covered, for up to 12 hours. Cook steaks on grill (doesn't take long—don't overdo). Fry onions separately in a frying pan and serve over steaks. Good served with pork and beans.

LOIS BANASCH
Bow Island, Alberta

SOUTHWEST SWEET AND SOUR ELK

3 pounds short ribs or elk meat

Garlic salt

Lemon pepper

Flour

1 large red onion, sliced thin

2 tablespoons butter (or oil)

2 tablespoons Worcestershire sauce

¼ cup bottled chili sauce

1 teaspoon chili powder

¼ cup ketchup (or sweet chili sauce)

1 cup red wine

½ cup red wine vinegar

1 cup brown sugar

Sprinkle meat with garlic salt and lemon pepper. Dredge in flour. Sauté onion in butter until translucent and remove from pan. Add more butter or oil as needed to brown meat. Transfer meat and onions to large casserole.

In a bowl mix all other ingredients together. Pour over meat, cover with lid or foil, and bake for 3 hours at 325°F–350°F. Check periodically and add more wine or water as necessary. Serve with egg noodles or polenta.

RICHARD DIMBAT
Bend, Oregon

VENISON BACON PARMESAN

2 strips bacon

1 tablespoon cooking oil

2 venison steaks (¼ inch thick is ideal)

½ cup Parmesan salad dressing

1 teaspoon fresh horseradish

2 garlic cloves, minced (or ½ teaspoon powdered garlic)

4 teaspoons grated Parmesan cheese

Seasoned salt and pepper to taste

Put cooking oil and bacon strips in a large frying pan. Cook bacon till crisp, then remove and set aside. Add steaks to pan and brown on both sides. Crumble the strips of bacon and add them plus all remaining ingredients to a small bowl and stir. Add half of the mixture to the steak side that's up, then turn steak over and add the remaining ingredients to the other side. Cook steaks 2 minutes more on each side or until done. Remove steaks from frying pan. Stir sauce in pan until it starts to thicken. Pour sauce over steaks and serve.

EDWARD J. FLEMING
Sergeantsville, New Jersey

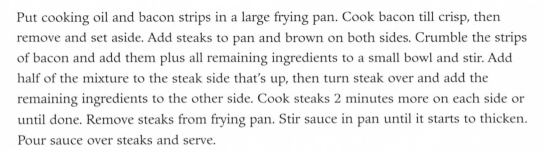

VENISON SAN MARCO

1–1½ pounds venison, moose, or elk steaks, cut into serving pieces
1 envelope onion soup mix
1 pound diced tomatoes in juice
1 teaspoon dried oregano
Garlic powder to taste (generous amount)
Salt and pepper to taste
2 tablespoons olive oil
2 tablespoons red wine vinegar

Arrange meat in a large skillet. Sprinkle with meat tenderizer if desired. Cover with soup mix and tomatoes. Sprinkle with remaining ingredients. Cover and simmer 1 hour. Serve over rice or boiled potatoes. Serves 3 to 4.

MARY ANNE LECCE
Collinsville, Illinois

VENISON "WHITE WINE" STEAKS

½ cup white wine
½ can beer
¾ cup soy sauce
2 cloves garlic
2 teaspoons white sugar
½ teaspoon ground ginger
Seasoned salt and pepper to taste
4 venison steaks (¼ inch thick is best) (can substitute other game meat)
½ cup 7 Up

Combine first seven ingredients in a bowl. Place steaks in marinade and let them sit overnight in the refrigerator. Take out steaks and cook them to desired doneness. Pour remaining juices back into pan. Now add 7 Up and mix. Bring to a boil while stirring often. After mixture has thickened, pour over steaks or use as a gravy.

EDWARD J. FLEMING
Sergeantsville, New Jersey

VENISON SWISS STEAK

8 venison steaks

Salt and pepper to taste

3 tablespoons bacon grease (or olive oil)

2 cloves garlic, smashed and chopped fine

½ green bell pepper, chopped into small pieces

½ onion, chopped into small pieces

2–4 stalks of celery, chopped

1 small can mushrooms, drained

1 15½-ounce can whole tomatoes (hot Rotel tomatoes suggested)

1 15½-ounce can diced tomatoes

1 small can tomato paste

1 can or bottle beer

Trim all silver skin or any bad looking portion from the venison, then salt and pepper both sides to taste. Heat bacon grease in a deep pan or pot. When the grease is melted, add the garlic and brown it. Next add the venison and brown it, but do not overcook. Remove the venison when browned and place it on a plate. Now add the green pepper, onion, and celery to cook them until the onion is translucent but not done all the way. Add mushrooms, tomatoes, and tomato paste. Rinse the cans with some of the beer, then add the rest. Bring to a slow boil and put the venison back in. Continue to cook until meat is tender, about 1–1½ hours. Test with a fork. If you want the sauce a little thicker, add a little cornstarch and water mixture. Serve over mashed potatoes or rice and wash it down with a good bottle of your favorite wine.

You can substitute round steak or any other wild game—elk, caribou, moose, etc. This can also be done with grouse and served over pasta.

TOM LUKOWICZ
Bartonville, Texas

BAKED SWISS STEAK
WITH VEGETABLES

2 pounds trimmed boneless elk or deer roast (may substitute
    buffalo or beef)

1 tablespoon each oregano, thyme, and garlic salt

Fresh-ground pepper and nutmeg to taste

1 cup flour

1 tablespoon paprika

1 large onion, halved and sliced

24 medium or large mushrooms

2 tablespoons each bacon grease, butter, and olive oil

¼ cup red wine

2 tablespoons beef bouillon granules

1½ cups hot water

6 medium red potatoes, unpeeled and halved

6 large carrots, peeled and halved

Trim all fat and cut roast against grain into eight or more ½-inch steaks. Lay steaks
flat on board and sprinkle lightly with half the oregano, thyme, and garlic salt and
dust with pepper and nutmeg. Gently pound the steaks with a metal meat tenderizer
to flatten them and drive the seasonings into the meat. Duplicate the process on the
other sides.

Dredge and completely cover each steak side with flour mixed with paprika. Line
the bottom of a large covered roasting pan with half the onions and 8 mushrooms
cleaned and quartered.

In a large skillet brown the floured steaks for 3–5 minutes per side in the
medium-hot bacon grease, butter, and olive oil. After the steaks are browned, place
them on top of the sliced onions and mushrooms in the roasting pan. Deglaze the

skillet by adding the remainder of the sliced onions and stir for several minutes until they begin to wilt. Add the wine and stir for another minute. Smother the steaks with the sliced onions and wine mixture. Dissolve the bouillon granules in the hot water and pour it over the steaks and cover with lid. Place in a 325°F preheated oven and bake for 70 minutes.

Halve the remaining mushrooms. Distribute the potatoes, carrots, and mushroom halves cut-side down evenly on top of the steaks and bake for another 45–60 minutes, until potatoes and carrots are cooked but firm to the touch when pierced with a fork. Do not overcook. When done, remove from oven and let stand covered for 10–15 minutes to allow juices to rehydrate the meat and thicken the gravy. Slightly mash the cooked potatoes on each plate and top with butter or margarine and gravy juices. Serves 6.

BILL ROMPA
Albany, Oregon

Brisket with Mushrooms

For 4½ pounds of deer or boar brisket, use 3½ ounces lard or shortening, 2 slices bacon, about 2 pounds mushrooms, pepper, and salt. Sprinkle brisket with salt and pepper, then fry in fat until browned. In a saucepan place bacon strips and browned meat and top with mushrooms. (Leave smaller mushrooms whole, halve larger ones.) Pour a half cup of hot water over meat, add a pinch more pepper and salt, and cook covered over a low flame for about an hour. Place meat on platter, decorate with cooked mushrooms. Strain sauce and pour over meat.

VADIM RIBAKOV
Smolensk, Russia

Broiled Backstrap Steaks

This recipe is simple and fast. It is really only for the best cuts of venison or elk, especially the backstraps. I cut backstrap steaks across the grain, butterfly style, with the first cut nine-tenths of the way through, then the next cut all the way through. The closer you get to either end of the strap, there's more connective tissue, which needs to be trimmed off if you want to keep them top quality. I look at each steak and grade it when I wrap it, A+ down to B-, so I know what I'm serving. This recipe works for everything down to the Bs (many of which will come out of the various cuts of ham, as well as the very best of the shoulder if they are cut just right).

Turn the broiler on and let it get as hot as it's going to get. Take a big frying pan or an oven-safe dish and brush it with olive oil. Lay the steaks down so they do not overlap each other. You can brush them with olive oil if you are going to put them on the topmost rack of the oven, right under the broiler, which is the best way. Rub them with a couple of cloves of garlic crushed in a garlic press. Sprinkle with a few pinches of powdered mustard and two short shots of Worcestershire sauce on each one, if you desire. Add some fresh ground black pepper and crushed fresh rosemary. None of this is slathered on—each ingredient is used in just enough quantity to bring out the flavor of the meat, not change it.

Use the top rack, and slide the pan under the broiler. There will be smoke. Turn on the exhaust fan. Don't leave the room, and don't pour drink number six and start talking about elk hunting politics or any other dark subjects. Vigilance is the absolute rule here. It is a sin to turn quality wild game steaks into husks.

At 5 or 6 minutes, start thinking about taking the steaks out. I've never gotten the steaks just right without taking them out and cutting into one to see how done it is.

Remember that the steaks keep on cooking—really keep on cooking—after you take them out of the oven, because the pan is so hot. I've ruined them by taking them out just as they got done, and then leaving them to overcook on the counter, still in the pan.

After you take the steaks out of the pan, you can pour some red wine or water in the pan and make au jus out of the drippings (add some salt now), and use that to reconstitute some dried morels and pour the whole mess over French bread.

HAL HERRING
Corvallis, Montana

PEPPER STEAK

2½ pounds venison steaks
Flour for dredging
Salt and pepper to taste
3 tablespoons olive oil
2 cubes beef bouillon
2 cups boiling water
2 tablespoons soy sauce

1 tablespoon Worcestershire
   sauce
1 teaspoon onion salt
1 teaspoon garlic salt
1 small can mushrooms
2 fresh tomatoes, cubed
½ green pepper, cubed

Pound flour, salt, and pepper into steak. Cut meat into strips about 1 inch wide. Brown in olive oil. Dissolve bouillon cubes in 2 cups boiling water. Add soy sauce, Worcestershire sauce, onion salt, and garlic salt. Pour over meat and simmer about ½ hour. Add mushrooms, tomatoes, and green pepper 15 minutes before serving. Serves 8.

SUZETTE HORTON
Idaho Falls, Idaho

Barbecued Cottontail Rabbit

Cut rabbit in serving pieces and place in casserole. Pour a small amount of barbecue sauce on each piece. Sprinkle with Italian spaghetti seasoning. Bake at 275°F for about 2 hours until done.

BILL BAILEY
Elizabeth, Colorado

ELK SCALLOPINI

4 heaping tablespoons flour
1 tablespoon seasoned salt
1 tablespoon black pepper
4–6 elk steaks, tenderized
6 tablespoons olive oil
½ onion, thinly sliced
2 3-ounce cans mushrooms
1 tablespoon capers, drained
1 tablespoon garlic
2 tablespoons dried oregano
2 tablespoons dried basil
1 tablespoon dried thyme
1 15½-ounce can diced tomatoes
1 package egg noodles
2 tablespoons butter

Mix flour, seasoned salt, and pepper. Dredge steaks in flour mixture and lightly brown them in hot oil. Remove and add onion to pan. Cook until tender. Return meat to pan and add remaining ingredients except noodles. Cover and simmer for 20 minutes, stirring occasionally. After 15 minutes prepare noodles. Drain and add 2 tablespoons butter into noodles until melted. Place steak on noodles and top with pan sauce.

MICHAEL POOR
Yakima, Washington

VENISON (OR MOOSE OR ELK) SCALLOPINI MARSALA

1 pound venison, moose, or elk fillets,
    ¼ inch thick
Meat tenderizer (if desired)
Salt and pepper to taste
1 egg
3 tablespoons milk
⅔ cup seasoned bread crumbs
2 tablespoons Parmesan cheese
4 tablespoons butter

1 tablespoon chopped garlic
8 ounces fresh mushrooms,
    sliced
½ cup green pepper, sliced in very thin
    short strips
1 beef bouillon cube
1 cup water
2 teaspoons flour
¼–½ cup Marsala wine (to taste)

Sprinkle fillets with meat tenderizer, salt, and pepper. Puncture meat lightly with a fork. Mix egg, milk, salt, and pepper in a shallow bowl. Combine bread crumbs and Parmesan cheese in another bowl. Dip fillets in egg mixture and then coat with bread crumb mixture. Melt 2 tablespoons butter in skillet over medium heat. Add garlic and fillets. Cook over medium heat, turning, until fillets are light brown. Remove to heated platter. Keep warm.

Melt remaining 2 tablespoons butter in the skillet. Sauté mushrooms and green pepper over medium heat until tender. Dissolve bouillon cube in water. Add flour. Mix well. Add with Marsala wine to mushrooms and green peppers. Simmer on low until thickened. Pour over steaks. Serves 4.

Variation: Substitute white wine and a splash of cognac (up to ¾ cup) for Marsala wine. Add one diced fresh tomato, peeled and seeded, to the mushrooms and substitute ½ cup chopped canned artichoke hearts for green pepper.

MARY ANNE LECCE
Collinsville, Illinois

ELK STROGANOFF

1 package frozen home-style noodles or dried noodles
4 elk steaks, sliced into strips
Cooking oil
Salt and pepper
1–2 cans cream of mushroom soup
1 10-ounce package frozen peas
Extra mushrooms (optional)

Prepare noodles according to the package directions. While the noodles are cooking, fry the elk strips in just enough oil to cook them. Add salt and pepper to taste. When the noodles are ready, drain, and add the meat, soup, and frozen peas and mushrooms if desired. Add water to make gravy desired consistency. Heat until bubbling and the peas are hot.

ELIZABETH HILL
Show Low, Arizona

VENISON STROGANOFF

1½ pounds of venison (moose, elk, duck, or goose or dove breasts
    can be substituted)

⅓ cup flour (seasoned with salt and pepper and a dash of nutmeg)

4 tablespoons butter

1 tablespoon chopped garlic

1 cup chopped onions

8 ounces fresh mushrooms, sliced

Salt and pepper to taste

Juice from ½ fresh lemon

1 teaspoon Worcestershire sauce

1 cup water

1 beef bouillon cube

½ cup white wine or sherry

1 cup sour cream (fat-free works fine)

Slice the meat very thin, diagonally and coat with seasoned flour. Brown in butter
and garlic in skillet (to cut fat, start with 1 tablespoon butter and add more only as
needed). Add onions and mushrooms and continue sautéing on low heat until
onions and mushrooms are tender, stirring frequently to avoid sticking. (If you cover
skillet while browning ingredients, they will stay moister and require less butter.) Add
salt and pepper to taste. Squeeze juice of ½ lemon over onion and mushrooms while
cooking. Add Worcestershire sauce, water, beef bouillon cube, and wine. Simmer,
covered, for 45–60 minutes. Stir in sour cream. (You can eliminate the sour cream if
you want a darker gravy.) Cook until just heated through. Serve over noodles. Serves
4 to 6.

MARY ANNE LECCE
Collinsville, Illinois

WEST TEXAS FRIED VENISON

¼ cup flour

1 teaspoon salt

1 teaspoon pepper

2 pounds venison, cut into serving sizes

3 teaspoons olive oil

1 stalk celery, sliced

3 onions, sliced into rings

1 tablespoon Worcestershire sauce

2 cups chopped tomatoes

Mix flour, salt, and pepper together. Coat venison with flour mixture, heat olive oil, and brown venison on both sides. Add celery and onions and brown. Add Worcestershire sauce and tomatoes and cook, covered, for 1–2 hours (depending on age of animal) or until tender. Serve over steaming noodles. Serves 4.

SUZETTE HORTON
Idaho Falls, Idaho

VENISON (OR MOOSE OR ELK) OR DUCK PARMESAN

1 pound venison, moose, or elk fillets, sliced ¼ inch thick
    (duck or goose breasts may be substituted)
Meat tenderizer (if desired)
Salt and pepper to taste
1 egg
3 tablespoons milk
⅔ cup seasoned bread crumbs
2 tablespoons grated Parmesan cheese
2 tablespoons butter
1 tablespoon chopped garlic
Tomato sauce
Grated mozzarella cheese

Sprinkle fillets with meat tenderizer (if desired), salt, and pepper. Puncture meat lightly with a fork. Mix egg, milk, salt, and pepper in a shallow bowl. Combine bread crumbs and Parmesan cheese in another shallow bowl. Dip fillets in egg mixture and then coat with bread crumb mixture.

Melt butter in skillet. Add garlic and fillets. Cook over medium heat, turning, until fillets are light brown. Place fillets in shallow baking dish. Cover each fillet with a small amount of tomato sauce. Sprinkle with grated mozzarella cheese. Bake in a 300°F oven until cheese melts. Serve with spaghetti. Serves 4.

MARY ANNE LECCE
Collinsville, Illinois

CROCK-POT STEAK AND STUFFING

2 pounds elk or venison steak, sliced about ¼ inch thick
1 box pork stuffing mix
1 can golden mushroom soup
1 teaspoon salt and pepper seasoning

Prepare stuffing mix and season steak to your taste. Place a layer of steak in Crock-Pot, followed by a layer of stuffing. Repeat until all of the stuffing and steak is gone. I like to start and end with a layer of steak. Pour soup over top of last layer. Don't add water. Cook on low for about 3–5 hours or high for about 2–3 hours, or until meat is tender.

PAUL G. DAVIS
Westfield, Pennsylvania

Webster's Tender (Game) Vittles

In a large (clay) uncovered pot, place 1 large sliced onion on the bottom. Then, place 4–6 peppercorns, diced garlic cloves (to taste), 1 tablespoon salt, 3 bay leaves, ¼ pound diced bacon, and 4–5 pounds of fat-trimmed, chunk-cut meat. Add a bottle of wine (use blush or rosé for poultry and red for beef or game), then fill pot with water.

Bake at 400°F for 1 hour. Then turn down heat to 250°F and bake for another 8 hours. Add water as it cooks down. Bake less time for poultry.

Serve meat with "juice" over rice. This tastes even better the next day.

BRIAN R. WEBSTER
Englewood, Colorado

ORIENTAL VENISON (OR MOOSE OR ELK)

⅓ cup teriyaki marinade and sauce

¼ cup soy sauce

1 tablespoon chopped garlic

1 teaspoon crumbled Italian herb seasoning

1 teaspoon ground ginger

½ teaspoon cayenne pepper

1 teaspoon seasoned salt

1 teaspoon seasoned pepper (such as garlic pepper)

1 teaspoon ground mustard

1 teaspoon olive oil

1 jalapeño pepper, diced fine

1 medium onion, sliced vertically

1 medium zucchini, sliced thin

1 medium yellow squash, sliced thin

1½ pounds venison, moose, or elk, sliced thin, diagonally

½ pound fresh mushrooms, quartered

1 small can sliced water chestnuts (optional)

2 tablespoons cornstarch

¼ cup dry white wine

Combine all ingredients except mushrooms, water chestnuts, cornstarch, and wine. Marinate meat overnight in a nonmetal container.

Spray wok with cooking spray. Cook meat, vegetables, and marinade until meat is browned and vegetables tender (approximately 10–15 minutes). Add mushrooms and simmer for 5 minutes. Add water chestnuts (if desired). Mix cornstarch and white wine until smooth. Add to wok. Simmer until thickened. Serve over noodles or rice.

This is also good with duck, goose, or chicken.

MARY ANN LECCE
Collinsville, Illinois

SATAY-STYLE VENISON (OR MOOSE OR ELK)

⅓ cup teriyaki marinade and sauce

2½ tablespoons creamy peanut butter

1 teaspoon cornstarch

1½ pounds venison, moose, or elk, sliced thin (duck or goose may be used)

1 teaspoon ground ginger

½ teaspoon cayenne pepper

1 teaspoon seasoned salt

1 teaspoon seasoned pepper (such as garlic pepper)

1 tablespoon chopped garlic

½–1 pound snow pea pods (frozen is fine)

½ pound fresh mushrooms, quartered

4 green onions, sliced

1 15-ounce can chicken broth

1 small can sliced water chestnuts

In a small bowl combine teriyaki sauce, peanut butter, and cornstarch. Whisk until smooth and well blended. Season meat with ground ginger, cayenne pepper, seasoned salt, and seasoned pepper. Spray wok with cooking spray. Heat wok. Add garlic and meat. Brown meat. Add snow peas, then cover and simmer about 5 minutes. Add sauce mixture, mushrooms, and green onions. Cover and simmer about 5 minutes. Thin sauce with chicken broth (only as much as needed, not the whole can) and add water chestnuts. Cook until just heated through. Serve over noodles. Serves 4 to 6.

MARY ANNE LECCE
Collinsville, Illinois

ELK "OLIVES"

1½ pounds boned elk or moose

1 tablespoon unsweetened mustard
    or Strong Swedish Mustard (see
    page 195)

2 slices bacon or salt pork

Salt and pepper to taste

1 large gherkin (deli-size)

1 onion, sliced

Butter for frying

1 cup water

1 beef bouillon cube

1 tablespoon flour

¼ cup whipping cream

2 pounds new potatoes

Mushrooms

Slice the meat into 8 medium-thick fillets. Place fillets in plastic bag and pound to flatten. Brush the fillets with mustard. Divide the bacon or salt pork into 8 pieces and place one on each slice. Sprinkle with salt and pepper. Divide the pickled gherkin lengthwise into 4 pieces, then cut each in half at the middle. Place one piece of the pickled gherkin and some onion on each of the fillets. Roll the fillets partly around the stuffing, fold in the ends, and then continue rolling them up. Insert a toothpick into each "olive" to retain their shape.

Brown olives on all sides in butter in a frying pan. When done, place olives in a saucepan. Add water and a crumbled beef bouillon cube. Braise on low heat for 30–60 minutes or until meat is tender.

Meanwhile wash and boil potatoes with the skin on. Clean mushrooms and cut into large pieces. Brown them in butter.

Take out the olives, remove toothpick, and keep them hot, while you prepare the sauce. Heat the liquid in the saucepan, and mix in 1 tablespoon butter and 1 tablespoon flour. Add whipping cream and blend. Place 2 olives and serving of mushrooms on a plate. Add some sauce and a serving of potatoes.

A. J. CHRISTIANSEN
Kimball, Nebraska

VENISON IN RICE

1 small box quick-cooking rice
1 small onion, chopped
6 venison chops
1 can cream of celery soup
1 can cheese soup
1 cup milk
1 package dry onion soup mix
1 10-ounce package frozen broccoli spears, thawed

Preheat oven to 350°F. Sprinkle the rice in a buttered casserole dish. Place venison chops on the layer of rice and sprinkle the chopped onions over the chops. Mix the can soups with the milk and pour over the chops. Sprinkle the dry onion soup mix over the entire casserole and place the broccoli spears over that. Cover with foil and bake for 2 hours in the preheated oven.

BRENT BACON
Lewisburg, Pennsylvania

VENISON WITH SOUR CREAM

2 pounds cubed venison or elk
¼ cup cooking oil
1 clove garlic
1 cup diced celery
1 bay leaf
4 tablespoons butter
2–2½ cups water
4 beef bouillon cubes
1 cup diced carrots
1 teaspoon salt
4 tablespoons flour
1 cup sour cream

Brown cubed meat in oil with garlic. Put in Crock-Pot with all other ingredients except flour and sour cream. Cook all day in Crock-Pot. About 1 hour before serving, mix sour cream with flour. Add some hot juices from the pot and stir well. Add mixture to Crock-Pot and cook until slightly thickened. Serve over noodles or spaetzle.

BARB TROCHTA
West Yellowstone, Montana

VENISON (OR MOOSE OR ELK) PAPRIKA

2 pounds cubed venison, moose, or elk (also good with duck or goose)

½ teaspoon meat tenderizer (optional)

1½ tablespoons flour

½ teaspoon seasoned salt

¼ teaspoon pepper

¼ teaspoon garlic powder

2 tablespoons olive oil

3 cloves garlic, mashed

1 large onion, sliced lengthwise

1½ tablespoons paprika (can use mixture of hot and sweet paprika)

⅛ teaspoon nutmeg

1 tablespoon tomato paste

1 beef bouillon cube

½ cup water

½ cup port wine

8 ounces fresh mushrooms, quartered

Sprinkle meat with meat tenderizer (if desired). Combine flour, seasoned salt, pepper and garlic powder in a plastic bag. Add cubed meat. Close and shake to coat meat with flour mixture. Brown meat in olive oil in a large skillet. Add remaining ingredients (except mushrooms) and simmer, covered, for 45 minutes. Add mushrooms and simmer, uncovered, for another 15 minutes. Serve with noodles. Serves 4.

MARY ANNE LECCE
Collinsville, Illinois

SWEET AND SOUR ELK

3 pounds elk roast, cut into cubes
2 tablespoons cooking oil
1 package dry onion soup mix
2 cups water
¼ cup ketchup
½ cup brown sugar
½ cup vinegar

Brown meat in oil. Sprinkle dry onion soup over meat. Combine and add remaining ingredients. Place in Crock-Pot and cook on low for 8 hours. Serve over rice or noodles. Serves 4.

LESLIE COLLAR
Bailey, Colorado

CROCK-POT VENISON AND MUSHROOMS

3 pounds venison, cut into 1-inch
    cubes, or drained canned
    venison
¾ cup red wine
1 package dry onion soup mix
1 can golden mushroom soup
1 can cream of mushroom soup
1–3 cups fresh or canned sliced
    mushrooms

Put everything together in the Crock-Pot, mix it up, and cook for about 10–12 hours on a low setting, then on high for about 1 hour. Serve over noodles, rice, or potatoes. For some added zing, you can top with sour cream before serving.

BRENT BACON
Lewisburg, Pennsylvania

ELK AND POTATOES

Oil for frying
2 pounds elk meat
Garlic powder
Seasoned salt
Pepper
Italian seasoning
7 beef bouillon cubes
7 cups water
Flour
8 potatoes

Put a half inch of oil in bottom of frying pan. Brown elk, adding garlic powder, seasoned salt, pepper, and Italian seasoning. Remove meat from pan, saving drippings. In separate pan, boil 7 bouillon cubes in 7 cups water until dissolved. Pour into drippings pan, then add a little flour and mix until it thickens into a gravy. Cube potatoes and boil. Add meat to gravy and pour over potatoes. Serve with corn on the cob and enjoy. Beer is optional but adds that extra little taste.

JERRY ELLARD
Loveland, Colorado

ELK KABOBS

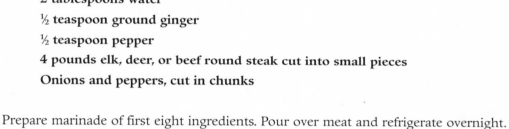

½ teaspoon garlic powder

¼ cup soy sauce

1 teaspoon meat tenderizer

1 tablespoon brown sugar

1 tablespoon oil

2 tablespoons water

½ teaspoon ground ginger

½ teaspoon pepper

4 pounds elk, deer, or beef round steak cut into small pieces

Onions and peppers, cut in chunks

Prepare marinade of first eight ingredients. Pour over meat and refrigerate overnight. Remove meat from marinade. Alternate meat, onion, and peppers on skewers. Cook on grill.

VERLIN FUNKHOUSER
Paris, Illinois

ELK (OR DEER OR MOOSE) OVEN STEW

1 pound elk, venison, or moose cut into 1-inch cubes (beef also
  may be used)
1 teaspoon salt
¼ teaspoon pepper
1 teaspoon garlic powder (or more based on your taste)
1 teaspoon paprika (or more based on your taste)
1 teaspoon meat tenderizer (optional)
1 10-ounce can tomato soup
10 ounces water
1 tablespoon sugar
2 tablespoons tapioca
2 medium onions, sliced
1 cup chopped celery
2 cups chopped carrots
4 medium potatoes, peeled and cut in large cubes

Place meat in a heavy, ovenproof casserole. Sprinkle with salt, pepper, garlic powder, paprika, and meat tenderizer (if desired). Mix tomato soup, water, sugar, tapioca, and vegetables. Pour over meat. Cover and bake at 300°F for 4 hours. Serves 4.

MARY ANNE LECCE
Collinsville, Illinois

WATCHAGOT STEW

4 14½-ounce cans diced tomatoes

1 cup water

2 bay leaves

1 beef bouillon cube

1½ teaspoons dried oregano

3 cloves garlic, chopped

2 teaspoons salt

1 teaspoon pepper

2 tablespoons sugar

3 pounds cubed wild meat (such as
   venison, moose, or elk) or 2 rabbits,
   cleaned and cut into pieces, or 3
   squirrels, cleaned and cut into
   pieces, or an equivalent amount of
   quail or dove—or whatever ya got
   on hand!

⅓ cup flour

1 teaspoon salt

½ teaspoon pepper

2 tablespoons olive oil

2 large onions, sliced

3 large potatoes, cubed

2 stalks celery, chopped

3 large carrots, sliced

3 tablespoons flour

½ cup cold water

Combine first nine ingredients in a heavy, large pan and simmer, covered, for 1 hour.

Dredge meat in flour seasoned with salt and pepper. Brown meat in olive oil. Add onions and cook until onions are tender (10 minutes). Combine with tomato mixture and simmer, uncovered, until meat is tender (about 2 hours).

Add potatoes, celery, and carrots to stew and simmer, uncovered, for 30–45 minutes or until vegetables are tender. Mix 3 tablespoons flour with ½ cup cold water. Stir until smooth. Add to stew and simmer until slightly thickened. Season to taste with salt and pepper.

MARY ANNE LECCE
Collinsville, Illinois

FAJITAS

6 ounces lime juice

3 cloves garlic, crushed

1 teaspoon cumin

1½ teaspoons each paprika, oregano, and cayenne pepper

¼ cup dehydrated onion flakes

1 teaspoon seasoned salt

¼–½ teaspoon red pepper flakes (optional)

½ cup dry white wine or sherry

2 tablespoons olive oil

2 pounds deer, moose, or elk steaks sliced ¼ inch thick, or duck or goose
    breasts, sliced thin horizontally

2 onions, sliced

1 red pepper, sliced

1 green pepper, sliced

1 tablespoon olive oil

Flour tortillas

Sour cream, salsa, and guacamole

Mix marinade of the first nine ingredients in a nonmetal container. Puncture meat all over with a fork and marinate for 5–6 hours or overnight. Grill quickly on a barbecue grill over a HOT flame, basting with the marinade. Sauté onions and peppers in 1 tablespoon olive oil in a skillet until cooked but not brown (approximately 10 minutes).

Wrap meat and vegetables in flour tortillas and top with sour cream, salsa, and guacamole. Serves 4.

MARY ANNE LECCE
Collinsville, Illinois

VENISON (OR MOOSE OR ELK) BOURGUIGNON

1½–2 pounds venison, moose, or elk, cubed

Salt and pepper to taste

Meat tenderizer (if desired)

2 tablespoons olive oil

1 tablespoon chopped garlic

1½ cups chopped onions or 6 ounces pearl onions

4 cups beef bouillon

1 tablespoon lemon juice

1 teaspoon Worcestershire sauce

2 bay leaves

1 tablespoon sugar

1 teaspoon paprika (hot or sweet)

Dash of ground cloves or allspice

½ cup sherry

½ cup dry red wine

4 carrots, cut into chunks

1 stalk celery, cut into chunks

2 medium potatoes, peeled and cubed, or 6 new potatoes, peeled

8–12 ounces fresh mushrooms, sliced

Season meat with salt and pepper (and meat tenderizer if desired). Brown in olive oil with garlic and onions. Add beef bouillon, lemon juice, Worcestershire sauce, and seasonings. Simmer for 1–2 hours, stirring occasionally. Add sherry, red wine, carrots, celery and potatoes. Cook for 15 minutes. Add mushrooms and cook 15 minutes longer or until vegetables are tender. Thicken cooking liquid for gravy with a paste of flour and water if desired. Serves 4 to 6.

MARY ANNE LECCE
Collinsville, Illinois

ELK OR VENISON CHILI

3½–4 pounds cubed (about ¾ inch) elk or venison
⅓ cup flour
1 teaspoon cumin
2–3 teaspoons chili powder
1 teaspoon each salt and pepper
1 teaspoon dried oregano
¼ cup cooking oil
4 tablespoons butter
2½ cups chopped onions
8 cloves garlic, crushed
2 cups beef stock
1 cup red wine
Sour cream, green onions, or shredded cheddar cheese

Roll cubes of elk or venison in a mixture of flour, cumin, chili powder, salt, pepper, and oregano. Set aside.

Place the oil and butter in a large skillet or pot (cast iron if possible). Add the chopped onions and half the crushed garlic to the skillet and brown. Remove the onions and garlic from the skillet and discard. Place the cubed elk in the skillet with some more oil and the other half of the crushed garlic and brown on all sides. Now add the beef stock and red wine to the elk cubes. Cover with a lid and bake at 275°F for 1 to 1½ hours. Garnish with sour cream, green onions, or shredded cheddar cheese.

JAMES PINCH
Spokane, Washington

ELKNUT'S CHILI

4 pounds elk steaks or roast, cut into
  ¼-inch cubes
3 tablespoons butter or margarine
¾ cup diced red or sweet onion
1 small can chiles, diced very fine
2 12-ounce cans chicken broth
9 tablespoons New Mexico chili powder
4 tablespoons ground cumin
1 tablespoon garlic powder

1 tablespoon paprika
1 tablespoon ground sage
2 teaspoons cayenne pepper
½ teaspoon powdered coriander
1½ tablespoons powdered beef soup
  base (or 8 crushed beef bouillon
  cubes)
2 tablespoons crushed red pepper

Trim away all fat and gristle from meat. (Hint: It's easier to cut the meat if it is very cold or slightly frozen.) Brown meat in skillet with 1 tablespoon of butter or margarine and transfer to a large pot when finished. Do not overcook! (Note: You will probably need to cook two batches unless your skillet is very large.) Sauté onions and chiles with 1 tablespoon butter or margarine and add to pot. Pour one can of chicken broth into pot. Cover and simmer at low heat.

Blend dry spices (except crushed red pepper) together in a mixing bowl. Add ¾ of the second can of chicken broth and mix into a paste. Spoon the spice mixture into the chili pot and use the remaining broth to rinse the leftover paste into the pot. Stir well until thoroughly mixed. Simmer at low heat for 2½ hours and stir occasionally, adding small amounts of water (or beer) as necessary to adjust consistency.

Place the crushed red pepper in a small piece of cheesecloth and tie securely with string (or use a tea strainer). Hang the pepper packet in the pot and remove when the desired degree of "heat" is achieved. Ladle into chili pots or hollowed-out sourdough bread loaves and sprinkle with grated cheese. Makes about 1½ gallons.

Remember: Anyone who knows beans about chili knows chili has no beans. This recipe may not be used in any sanctioned chili cook-off without written permission.

ANTHONY P. AUGUST
San Pedro, California

MOUNTAIN MAN CHILI

5 slices thick bacon, diced

1 pound hot Italian sausage links, sliced

1½ pounds elk stew meat, cubed

2 medium onions, chopped

3 cloves garlic, chopped

4 green Anaheim chiles, chopped

3 jalapeños, chopped

1½ tablespoons chili powder

½ teaspoon salt

1 12-ounce can tomato paste

1 10½-ounce can beef broth

10½ ounces black coffee

1 14½-ounce can stewed tomatoes

1 15½-ounce can kidney beans

1 15½-ounce can pinto beans

In a hot skillet fry the diced bacon until opaque. Remove bacon from the pan and set aside. Brown the sausage and cubed elk meat in the bacon fat and set aside.

Put the meat and all remaining ingredients except the beans in a large pot. Cover and simmer for 2 hours. Add the beans and simmer an additional 30 minutes, uncovered. Serve immediately with warm rolls and butter.

This chili is always a big hit at elk camp. I pack it in frozen and just heat it up after a long day in the field.

OWEN BRINKMANN
Aurora, Colorado

JACK'S SANDIA CHILI

2 pounds stew meat

1 dozen Hatch or Sandia chiles, peeled, seeded, and chopped

1 red bell pepper, cubed

1 small winter squash, cubed

1 teaspoon garlic powder (or minced fresh garlic)

1 teaspoon chili powder

1 pint turkey or pheasant stock, or beer

Juice from ½ lime

1 tablespoon chopped cooked bacon

2 10-ounce packages frozen corn, thawed (or equivalent fresh)

2–3 tablespoons masa (corn) flour

Brown meat and pour off fat. Add remaining ingredients, except corn and masa. Simmer for 1 hour or more. Add corn 10 minutes before serving. Mix masa in bowl with warm water, stir into a paste, then stir into chili. Serve in bowls and garnish with grated cheese. Serve with tortillas or corn bread.

JACK AND CHANTAL BUCHMILLER
Stamford, Connecticut

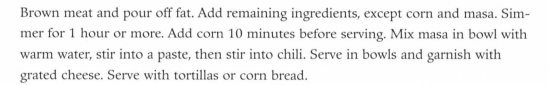

JACK'S GREEN CHILE STEW

5 pounds deer stew meat (this really fills the Crock-Pot; feel free
    to reduce portions)

¼ cup masa (corn) flour

Olive oil or clarified butter for frying

2 pounds fresh-frozen Hatch or Sandia chiles, peeled, seeded, and chopped

10 ounces frozen corn (or fresh)

4 teaspoons green Hatch chili powder

12 ounces lager beer

Take 1–2 pounds of the meat and shake in bag with masa flour (don't coat all the meat as that makes the taste of the corn flour overpowering). Brown the meat in olive oil or clarified butter. Add remaining ingredients. Simmer on low for 4 hours. Serve in bowls, garnished with grated cheese, served with tortillas or corn bread.

JACK AND CHANTAL BUCHMILLER
Stamford, Connecticut

JOHN'S NORTHWEST CHILI

6 ounces tomato paste

4 cups coarsely chopped canned or fresh tomatoes

5 cups beef broth

1 cup red wine

¼ cup apple cider vinegar

2 teaspoons chili powder (add more or less to suit taste)

2 teaspoons ground cumin

1 teaspoon ground oregano

1 teaspoon black pepper

3 tablespoons oil

2 pounds ground elk, venison, moose, etc.

2 large onions, coarsely chopped

1 head garlic, minced

1 green bell pepper, coarsely chopped

1 red bell pepper, coarsely chopped

4 cups fully cooked kidney beans

1 habañero pepper, finely chopped (optional, for medium-spicy flavor)

1 jalapeño pepper, finely chopped (optional, for medium-spicy flavor)

I prefer to use a 6-quart slow cooker. Combine tomato paste, tomatoes, broth, red wine, vinegar, and spices. Bring to a slow boil.

In a large skillet, heat 1½ tablespoons oil. Brown meat, then add meat to the slow cooker. Add the rest of the oil to the skillet and add the onions, garlic, bell peppers, beans, and optional hot peppers. Cook for 5 minutes to soften, and then add to the slow cooker. Cover and simmer for a minimum of 2 hours. I tend to let it cook for 6–8 hours to blend all of the flavors.

JOHN WORKMAN
Roy, Washington

RAY'S CHILI

6 slices bacon

1 pound sausage

1 pound wild game (elk or venison)

1–2 onions, chopped

1 bell pepper, chopped

4 cloves garlic, minced

2 chipotle peppers, diced (or substitute canned)

1 teaspoon dry mustard

4 tablespoons chili powder

¼ cup Worcestershire sauce

1 12-ounce bottle beer

1 28-ounce can tomatoes, chopped or mashed

2 15½-ounce cans kidney beans

Salt and pepper to taste

Brown bacon in a large pan that can be covered. Remove and crumble and set aside. Brown sausage in bacon fat. Remove sausage and set aside. Brown elk or venison and set aside. Cook onions, bell pepper, garlic, and chipotle peppers, simmering over low heat for about 5 minutes or until soft. Stir occasionally. Stir in mustard and chili powder and simmer 5 minutes. Add Worcestershire, beer, tomatoes, and meats. Bring to a boil, then reduce heat, cover, and simmer for 30 minutes. Add beans, heat again to boiling, then reduce heat and simmer 30 minutes. Season with salt and pepper to taste.

RAY SCHUTZ
Vandalia, Illinois

CHILI BUCK'S ELK CHILI

1 medium onion, chopped

2 stalks celery, chopped

1½ pounds ground elk

¼ cup olive oil

4 tablespoons chili powder

1 teaspoon salt

1 tablespoon garlic powder

1 teaspoon ground cumin

1 teaspoon marjoram

¼ teaspoon cayenne pepper

1 quart tomato juice

1 15½-ounce can red kidney beans, undrained

1 28-ounce can diced tomatoes, undrained

Sauté onion, celery, and ground elk in olive oil. Add the seasonings and stir until the mixture becomes an even red-brown color. Stir in the tomato juice and the kidney beans and diced tomatoes with their juices. Bring to a boil and add water if needed. Add cooked macaroni elbows or other cooked pasta if desired after meat mixture is done.

SANDY KRAMER
Waupaca, Wisconsin

QUICK ELK SKILLET ENCHILADAS

1 pound ground elk (try other ground meats too!)
½ cup chopped onion
1 can condensed cream of mushroom soup
1 10-ounce can enchilada sauce
⅓ cup milk
2 tablespoons chopped green chiles
Cooking oil
8 corn tortillas
2½ cups grated cheese
½ cup chopped olives

In skillet cook ground meat and onion until meat is brown and onion is tender; drain excess fat. Stir in soup, enchilada sauce, milk, and chiles. Reduce heat; cover and simmer 20 minutes, stirring occasionally.

In small skillet heat approximately ¼ inch oil. Dip tortillas in hot oil just until limp, about 5 seconds each side. Drain on paper towel. Fill each tortilla shell with cheese and olives, roll and place seam side down in ground meat mixture. Cover and cook until heated through. Sprinkle with cheese and continue cooking until cheese melts. Serve immediately with your favorite side dishes.

DIANA JENSEN
Post Falls, Idaho

ELK ENCHILADAS

1 pound ground elk
2 tablespoons cooking oil
1 large onion, chopped fine
1 tablespoon chili powder
Salt and pepper to taste
1 8-ounce can tomato sauce
2 cups water
1 can chili, without beans
1 dozen tortillas
Cooking oil for frying
1 pound cheddar cheese, grated

Brown meat in 2 tablespoons oil. Add ¼ cup onion, chili powder, and salt and pepper. Then add tomato sauce, 2 cups water, and chili. Simmer for 20 minutes.

Heat oil in skillet and dip tortillas in hot oil. Then fill each tortilla with 1 teaspoon onion, 2 tablespoons grated cheese, and 1 tablespoon chili mixture. Roll up and place seam-side down in casseroles. Top with additional onion, chili mixture, and grated cheese. Bake at 350°F for 20 minutes. Serve with Mexican rice or a salad.

JOHN R. HARVIEUX
Osceola, Wisconsin

VENISON ENCHILADAS

2 pounds ground venison, elk, bear, moose, or other wild game
    (beef can be substituted if you had an unlucky fall)
1 large onion, diced
2 cans chili beef with bean soup
1 large jar salsa (approximately 24 ounces)
8 large flour tortillas
½ pound cheddar cheese
1 head lettuce, chopped
2 tomatoes, chopped
2 medium jalapeño peppers, finely chopped
Sour cream

Brown meat with half of the diced onion. Drain and place in a large bowl. Add soup and half of the salsa. Gently stir until mixed well. It should have a thick, sticky consistency.

Grease or spray a 9-by-13-inch baking pan. Generously fill each tortilla with the meat mixture. Roll filled tortillas and place them in the baking pan tight to one another. Generally eight shells fill a pan. Set aside any remaining filling. Spread cheese over the top, leaving the outer edges of the shells exposed. Pour remaining salsa over cheese, making a line down the center. Cover with aluminum foil and place in a 350°F oven for 25 minutes. Then remove foil and bake, uncovered, another 5 to 7 minutes or so, until the edges of the shells are a light brown. Let sit for 5 minutes before serving. Top with chopped lettuce, tomato, onion, peppers, and sour cream. Any remaining filling makes great chip dip. Serves 4 to 6. They freeze very well.

ROBERT B. BARTECK
Wisconsin Rapids, Wisconsin

BBQ

1 bunch celery, chopped fine
Cooking oil
8 pounds ground elk, deer, or beef
2 pounds onions, chopped fine
4 28-ounce bottles ketchup
1 cup brown sugar
Salt and pepper to taste

Sauté celery in some cooking oil until tender and drain. Cook meat and onions together until done. Pour off grease. Add celery, ketchup, brown sugar, salt, and pepper. Simmer for at least 2 hours. Serve on hamburger buns.

VERLIN FUNKHOUSER
Paris, Illinois

Elk Neckbone Soup

Some of the best meat on an elk is from the neckbone. If you like soup, try this. When you get through cutting up your elk, take the neckbone after boning it out and saw it into 3-inch or 4-inch chunks. Place the chunks in a Dutch oven or stainless steel pot with an inch of water. Boil this on low for 2–3 hours, or until you can pull the meat off the bone with a fork. Remove bones to cool and start over with the same low heat to simmer chopped vegetables—carrots, spuds, celery, onions—in the liquid used to cook the bones. After a 2-hour slow boil, add the meat removed from the neckbones, along with salt, pepper, garlic powder, and chili powder. Use your favorite seasonings, but don't overdo it!! The best flavor is in the meat and vegetables. When done, add some honey and stir. I've never had a bad batch, and everyone wants more. Serve with corn bread or biscuits. For stew, do the same but with venison roast.

JACK LUTCH
Wickenburg, Arizona

PIE BURGERS

1 pound lean ground wild meat

½ package dry onion soup

⅓ cup pickle relish

4 tablespoons chili seasoning

2 teaspoons cumin (or substitute barbecue sauce)

½ cup evaporated milk, undiluted

2 teaspoons vinegar

2 cups flour

1 teaspoon salt

2 teaspoons caraway seeds

½ cup shredded cheddar cheese

⅔ cup shortening

Chili sauce

Brown meat with onion soup in skillet. Add relish, chili seasoning, and cumin.

Combine milk and vinegar in a cup. Sift flour and salt together into a bowl. Add caraway seeds and cheese to flour. Cut in shortening until particles are the size of small peas. Add milk mixture all at once and stir with a fork to moisten thoroughly to create a pastry dough.

Roll pastry out to form triangles for individual pies or make a bottom and top crust for one large pie. Fill pastry with meat filling. Bake at 425°F until crust is browned. Serve with chili sauce. Serves 8 to 10.

EDGAR AND MARJORIE RINEHART
Laramie, Wyoming

SAGUACHE PARK GOULASH

½ pound each ground antelope, elk or venison, hamburger, and pork sausage
Onion salt, garlic salt, and other seasonings to taste
2 16-ounce cans tomato sauce
Cooked pasta or noodles

Brown all meats together, then add seasonings and tomato sauce. Cook pasta or noodles, add to sauce, and let simmer until you are ready to eat. You can use fresh tomatoes or juice; just simmer longer to thicken if you do.

STEVEN E. BAILEY
Elizabeth, Colorado

Venison Stew

This recipe works best with a pressure cooker. Use enough meat as would make a good-size whitetail roast, but you can use tougher cuts from legs if pressure cooking. Cut into chunks 2-by-2 inches or thereabouts. Brown in bacon grease or oil in pressure cooker. Add 2 cubes beef bouillon, 2 large cloves squished garlic, 1 small diced onion, about ½ cup ketchup, about 1 tablespoon Italian seasoning, large cubes of potato, and large chunks of carrots. Cover with water, leaving enough room at top of cooker (2–3 inches). Seal and cook 14 minutes from the time the shaker starts to make noise. (If using a Crock-Pot, cook until tender.) Immediately run pressure cooker under cold water until pressure drops. Remove lid and scoop meat, potatoes, and carrots into big bowl. Replace gravy on burner. Place 3 heaping forkfuls of cornstarch into ½ cup cold water and stir. Add to hot gravy and stir until thickened. Pour over meat and veggies and serve.

HEATHER HARROD
Kentucky

ORIENTAL ELK SAUCE OVER SPAGHETTI

1 pound ground elk meat

½ cup chicken broth

⅓ cup hoisin sauce

¼ cup soy sauce

¼ cup beef broth

3 tablespoons minced onion

2 teaspoons minced garlic

1 teaspoon ground ginger

¼ teaspoon crushed red pepper

2 tablespoons cornstarch

16 ounces spaghetti, cooked and drained

1–2 teaspoons sesame oil (optional)

½ cup diagonally sliced green onions

Brown elk meat in large skillet and drain. In small bowl combine ¼ cup of the chicken broth, hoisin sauce, soy sauce, beef broth, minced onion, minced garlic, ground ginger, and crushed red pepper. Stir into elk meat in skillet, cover, reduce heat, and simmer for 10 minutes. In the meantime, dissolve cornstarch in the remaining ¼ cup chicken broth. Slowly stir into the meat mixture, then cook and stir until the sauce is thick.

In separate bowl, combine the spaghetti and sesame oil. Put spaghetti on serving platter and top with meat sauce and sliced green onions. Serves 4 to 6.

JOYCE SCHOLTEN
Dell Rapids, South Dakota

GRANDMA SUCCETTI'S ELK MEATBALLS

3 pounds ground elk meat

1 pound roll sausage

1 large can spinach, drained and squeezed dry

1 cup grated Parmesan cheese

1 cup Italian bread crumbs

½ bunch parsley, chopped fine

3 eggs

2 large white onions, chopped

Garlic salt, pepper, and salt to taste

Flour for dredging

Olive oil for frying

Mix first nine ingredients and roll into balls. Dredge meatballs in flour and fry in olive oil. Brown well all over and remove from pan.

TOMATO SAUCE

4 cloves garlic, chopped fine

1 large onion, chopped

½ bunch parsley, chopped fine

3 tablespoons olive oil

4 8-ounce cans tomato sauce

4 cups water

Sauté garlic, onion, and parsley in 3 tablespoons olive oil. Add tomato sauce and water and bring to a boil. Add meatballs and simmer for 2 hours, stirring carefully now and then.

KEVIN AND ANNETTE JOSEPH
Dolores, Colorado

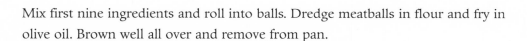

ELK MEATBALLS

1 pound ground elk

⅓ cup bread crumbs

1 egg

2 tablespoons steak sauce

2 tablespoons cooking oil

⅓ cup steak sauce

2 tablespoons brown sugar

2 tablespoons butter or margarine

Combine elk, bread crumbs, egg, and 2 tablespoons steak sauce. Mix and shape into 1-inch meatballs. Brown meatballs in oil in skillet. Drain fat from skillet. Combine ⅓ cup steak sauce, brown sugar, and butter with meatballs in skillet. Simmer, covered, for 15 minutes or until done. Makes about 2 dozen meatballs.

ARTHUR McMULLEN
Rector, Pennsylvania

KATE'S ITALIAN MEATBALLS

2 pounds ground meat (elk preferred)

2 cups Italian-style bread crumbs

1½ cups grated Parmesan cheese

½ teaspoon garlic powder

1 tablespoon parsley flakes

3 tablespoons onion flakes

Salt and pepper

7–8 eggs

4–8 cups spaghetti sauce (depending on your preference)

Mix all ingredients (except spaghetti sauce) together and form into balls. (It seems to work better if you put the eggs in near the end of the mixing process.) Brown the meatballs in a skillet. Remove them from the skillet and place them in a slow cooker or Crock-Pot. Cover them with spaghetti sauce and simmer for several hours. Serve over spaghetti and with bread. Makes enough for more than one meal. I find that my Crock-Pot is full with this recipe.

LYLE J. REGINNITTER
North Platte, Nebraska

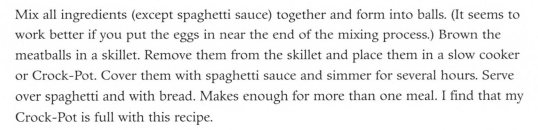

MONTANA PEPPER JACK TERIYAKI BURGERS

⅓ cup honey

⅓ cup soy sauce

4 cloves garlic, chopped

1 tablespoon grated fresh ginger

4 tablespoons sesame oil

1½ pounds venison burger

1 10-ounce can pineapple rings

1 red onion, sliced thin

Pepper Jack cheese, sliced

Combine honey, soy sauce, garlic, ginger, and sesame oil and mix well. In a large bowl pour sauce over meat and mix together. Form meat mixture into patties and cook on hot grill. When burgers are done, place one pineapple ring and onion slice on each burger. Top with cheese and let melt. Serve on fresh buns.

RYAN HANSON AND JIM WEBER
Helena, Montana

SEASONED ELK BURGERS

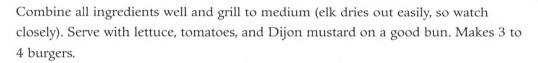

1 pound ground elk

1 egg

½ onion, minced (or 1 tablespoon dried minced onion)

1 large clove garlic, minced

3 tablespoons chopped fresh mint or 1 teaspoon dried mint

1 teaspoon ground cumin

½ teaspoon ground coriander

Combine all ingredients well and grill to medium (elk dries out easily, so watch closely). Serve with lettuce, tomatoes, and Dijon mustard on a good bun. Makes 3 to 4 burgers.

CAROL PETERSON
Colorado Springs, Colorado

Liver Snack Bar

Use one whole liver of elk, boar, or other game. For average 18 ounces of liver, add a half cup milk, 2 eggs, 1 ounce sifted flour, 3 cloves garlic, 2 slices bacon, 3 small onions (quartered), and ½ teaspoon each of baking soda, salt, pepper. Pass washed liver, bacon, and onions through meat grinder. Add salt, milk, eggs, and baking soda and mix. Spread meat mixture over greased baking sheet, and bake in medium oven until firm. Grease finished products with salted, crushed garlic.

VADIM RIBAKOV
Smolensk, Russia

OWEN'S ELK BURGERS
AND BLUE CHEESE

2 pounds of ground elk (mixed with about 2 ounces pork suet)

8 slices bacon

4 large onion rolls

1 jar blue cheese dressing

4 ounces blue cheese

Salt and pepper to taste

Tabasco sauce to taste

Divide the ground elk into four loosely packed burgers and set aside. In a large skillet fry the bacon until cooked but not crisp, then remove and set aside. Fry the elk burgers in bacon fat, turning only once, until medium rare. Place each burger on an open roll and spoon on the blue cheese dressing until the burger is covered. Add 2 slices of bacon to each burger, then, using a fork, crumble the blue cheese over the bacon. Add salt, pepper, and Tabasco to taste. Put the top of the roll on or serve open face. These go great with a frosty cold mug of your favorite ale.

OWEN BRINKMANN
Aurora, Colorado

MEAT LOAF

1 pound ground elk, deer, or beef

⅔ cup Bloody Mary mix

¼ cup chopped onion

1½ teaspoons salt

¼ teaspoon pepper

½ cup oats

3 tablespoons brown sugar

¼ teaspoon nutmeg

¼ cup ketchup

1 teaspoon dry mustard

Mix meat with Bloody Mary mix, onion, salt, pepper, and oats. Pack into a loaf shape on a baking pan. Combine brown sugar, nutmeg, ketchup, and dry mustard. Pour mixture over meat loaf. Bake at 350°F for 1–1½ hours until center is done.

VERLIN FUNKHOUSER
Paris, Illinois

BURICK'S 5-POUND ELK SALAMI

5 pounds ground elk (grind twice)

5 rounded teaspoons quick-cure salt

2½ teaspoons black pepper

⅛ teaspoon garlic powder

2 teaspoons hickory smoke salt

5 teaspoons white peppercorns
    (more if you like)

Mix all ingredients and put into a tightly covered bowl (not aluminum) and refrigerate for 3 days. Remove each day and mix thoroughly, as mixture will be very stiff.

After 3 days, separate mixture into five log rolls and place on ungreased cookie sheet. Cover with foil and return to refrigerator for 1 more day. Remove foil and place on cookie sheet in oven and bake for 12 hours at 125°F.

I suggest that salami be made in 10-pound batches.

R. J. BURICK
Los Alamos, New Mexico

RAG-A-DAS CAMP SUMMER SAUSAGE

5 pounds ground beef, elk, venison, or a mixture
2½ teaspoons coarsely ground pepper
2½ teaspoons whole mustard seed
2½ teaspoons garlic powder
5 rounded teaspoons quick-cure salt
1 teaspoon liquid smoke (omit if smoking sausage)

Combine all ingredients and mix well. Cover and refrigerate for 2 days. Remove from refrigerator, mix for 10 minutes, re-cover, and put back in refrigerator for 1 more day. Remove from refrigerator, mix for 10 minutes, and divide into loaves (5 pounds makes five loaves). Wrap loaves in plastic wrap and refrigerate overnight. Remove from refrigerator, remove plastic wrap, place on broiler pan, and bake at 140°F for 8 hours.

To cook in smoker, omit liquid smoke. Place on smoker racks and smoke overnight or approximately 13 hours.

SANDRA WATTERS
Orcas Island, Washington

GARLIC SAUSAGE

5 pounds ground game meat—elk, deer, moose, etc.

5 pounds ground unseasoned pork butt

3–5 tablespoons (mild, medium, hot) crushed red pepper flakes

1 tablespoon paprika

2–4 tablespoons (mild, garlicky, very garlicky) crushed garlic

5 tablespoons kosher salt

1 tablespoon ground black pepper

Up to 1 cup ice water, as needed

1 cup nonfat dry milk

Blend meats together and add remaining ingredients in order listed. Let stand in refrigerator overnight. Test sausage by cooking a small patty. Adjust seasoning if necessary. Package as desired.

TERRY LINDLEY
Bigfork, Montana

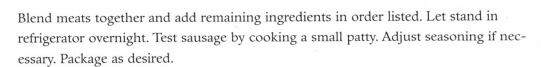

PORK SAUSAGE

3 pounds ground pork butt

¾–1 pound pork fatback, ground

4 tablespoons kosher salt

2 teaspoons coarsely ground
     black pepper

2 tablespoons dried sage

1 teaspoon dried thyme

2 teaspoons sugar

1 tablespoon red pepper flakes

1 teaspoon cayenne pepper

½ cup ice water

Blend meats together and add remaining ingredients in order listed. Let stand in refrigerator overnight. Test sausage by cooking a small patty. Adjust seasoning if necessary. Package as desired.

TERRY LINDLEY
Bigfork, Montana

Tasty Brisket

Marinate brisket for 2½ to 3 days in a refrigerator in even portions of Worcestershire sauce, soy sauce, wine, and liquid smoke. Wrap the marinated brisket in foil and cook at 200°F for 24 hours, or you may pressure cook for about 1 hour. You may substitute elk roast or other roast for brisket.

CAROL ALEXANDER
Montrose, Colorado

BIG SKY ITALIAN SAUSAGE

5 pounds ground venison

5 pounds ground pork

4 tablespoons kosher salt

2 tablespoons paprika

1½ tablespoons crushed red chili pepper

4 tablespoons whole fennel seeds

1 tablespoon ground coriander

2 tablespoons garlic granules

2 tablespoons lemon juice

1½ cups Parmesan cheese

1 14½-ounce can Italian-style stewed tomatoes, crushed

1 cup nonfat dry milk

1 cup ice water

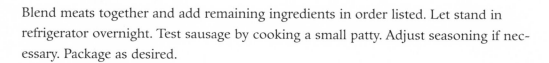

Blend meats together and add remaining ingredients in order listed. Let stand in refrigerator overnight. Test sausage by cooking a small patty. Adjust seasoning if necessary. Package as desired.

TERRY LINDLEY
Bigfork, Montana

GAME BREAKFAST SAUSAGE

5 pounds ground game (elk, deer, antelope, moose)

5 pounds ground pork, unseasoned

6 tablespoons kosher salt

1 tablespoon ground sage

1½ teaspoons ground ginger

1 tablespoon thyme

1 tablespoon nutmeg

1 tablespoon ground black pepper

1 cup nonfat dry milk

Blend meats together and add remaining ingredients in order listed. Let stand in refrigerator overnight. Test sausage by cooking a small patty. Adjust seasoning if necessary. Package as desired.

This is not really spicy. If you want a little heat, add 3–5 tablespoons (mild, medium, hot) crushed red pepper flakes.

TERRY LINDLEY
Bigfork, Montana

BREAKFAST CASSEROLE

1 32-ounce bag frozen hash browns (the chunk kind)

1 pound sausage, browned and crumbled (pork, turkey,
    game, Italian, breakfast, etc.)

1 pound Velveeta, cubed (do not substitute other cheese)

1 can cream of mushroom soup

⅔ cup milk

6 large eggs

1 teaspoon salt

½ teaspoon pepper

3 tablespoons dried parsley

3 tablespoons dried onion

Combine all ingredients in large bowl and pour into a deep 9-by-13-inch greased pan. Bake at 375°F until set—about 1¼–1½ hours.

This casserole can be baked and frozen, then thawed, cut in squares to serve, and reheated in a microwave. It can be frozen unbaked, left in the oven overnight with the automatic oven feature to come on so you wake up to a hot breakfast. Or it can be baked the morning you want to serve it and reheated as necessary in the microwave.

Variations: For vegetarian versions, omit sausage and add one 4-ounce can chopped green chiles and 8 ounces shredded cheese. The Mexican blend is very good. Bake as above and serve with fresh salsa. Other options are to add chopped green onions or chives; diced ham instead of sausage; additional cheese (whatever kind you like), shredded; or anything else that appeals to you.

CANDACE SPENCER
Littleton, Colorado

VENISON JERKY I

3 pounds lean venison

1 tablespoon salt

1 teaspoon onion powder

1 teaspoon garlic powder

1 teaspoon pepper

⅓ cup soy sauce

1 tablespoon prepared mustard

Cut venison (with the grain of the meat, not across the grain) into ½-inch wide and ½-inch thick strips. Mix all other ingredients and pour over meat. Marinate overnight. Remove meat from marinade and dry with paper towel. Place strips on cookie sheet in a single layer and dry at 200°F for 6–8 hours, or until dry. Cool and store in airtight sealed jar. Makes about 40 pieces.

RHONDA HORTON
Boise, Idaho

Venison Jerky II

It is recommended to freeze venison prior to making jerky, then thaw slightly before slicing. Slice venison against the grain in thin (⅛-inch) slices. Layer slices of venison, sprinkling of brown sugar, coarse ground black pepper, ground coriander, and coarse salt in container. Continue until done, ending with seasonings. Add mixture of ½ water and ½ distilled white vinegar until barely covered. Refrigerate and marinate three days, pouring off liquid as needed so meat remains barely covered. Place on trays in oven at very low heat and leave oven door open a crack while dehydrating until leathery, or use other drying methods. Seal tightly and refrigerate until needed.

HEATHER HARROD
Kentucky

GOOD JERKY RECIPE

1 tablespoon kosher salt

1 level teaspoon curing salt

1 teaspoon onion powder

1 teaspoon garlic powder

1 teaspoon ground black pepper

¼ cup soy sauce

⅓ cup Worcestershire sauce

3 pounds beef or venison, sliced with grain

Mix together all seasonings. Add meat and marinate in refrigerator overnight (stir 1 or 2 times). Drain. Dry in oven or smoker. After it's done, best to put in refrigerator in a resealable plastic bag. Then enjoy.

TERRY LINDLEY
Bigfork, Montana

JERKY MARINADE

⅛ cup salt

¼ cup sugar

2 cups water

½ cup soy sauce

½ cup Worcestershire sauce

½ cup teriyaki sauce

⅛ cup dry minced onion

4 cloves garlic, pressed

6 tablespoons brown sugar

1 shot whiskey (optional)

Meat cut in thin strips with the grain

Mix marinade ingredients together in a large bowl. Add meat. Cover with plastic wrap and let marinate overnight.

Take meat out of marinade and rinse. Lay onto racks in smoker. Sprinkle with lemon pepper if desired. Smoke over cherry wood for 3–4 hours, then heat cure for 5–7 hours or until done to taste.

Variations: For a tangier jerky, mix equal parts roasted garlic teriyaki and heated honey. After smoking is completed, baste mixture on jerky strips and continue with heat cure. This recipe can also be done in the oven at a low temperature (175°F–200°F). To get a smoky flavor, add 1 capful of liquid smoke. This will take 5–6 hours.

J. MATT TAGG
Nibley, Utah

TONGUE I

1 tongue
½ lemon, sliced
1 onion or 2 teaspoons onion salt
2 bay leaves
2 tablespoons cumin
2 teaspoons salt
Crushed pepper
4 cloves
2 tablespoons vinegar

Scrub tongue under warm water. Put all ingredients in pot of boiling water. Cover and simmer for 3–4 hours for slicing; cook all night for shredded tongue. Let cool in broth, then peel and trim gristle at base.

Use the broth to make soup. Add bouillon, veggies, beans, tomato, barley, garlic.

HEATHER HARROD
Kentucky

Tongue II

Boil the tongue until done. Peel outer covering off tongue while it's still hot. This will make that job much easier. Let the tongue thoroughly cool or chill. Cut into ¼- to ⅜-inch slices.

Place slices in bowl and pour in enough vinegar so that each slice or piece of tongue is at least partially submerged. Slice up an onion in the bowl and cover bowl with a leakproof lid. Shake bowl, turn upside down and shake to mix vinegar, onion, and tongue. Refrigerate overnight or about 8 hours before serving. Serve with crackers and a little salt and pepper if you want.

When I boil the tongue, I always slice an onion in the water and boil it along with the tongue. I discard this onion along with the water when tongue is finished boiling.

This recipe can be used with any tongue, such as elk, deer, beef, or pork. If you don't have a recipe for the heart of an animal that you consume, you can prepare the heart in the same manner as tongue. Trim fat from heart when preparing. If there is any left over in the vinegar, keep it refrigerated. You can snack on it for at least 2 weeks. It will keep that long easily.

ELWOOD STEIGERWALT
Andreas, Pennsylvania

BEST MINCEMEAT

2 pounds cooked venison or elk

¾ pound suet

4 pounds chopped apples

3 pounds currants and raisins

2 cups brown sugar (packed)

1½ teaspoon ground cinnamon

½ teaspoon ground cloves

½ teaspoon ground nutmeg

½ teaspoon allspice

2 teaspoons salt

2 quarts apple cider

1 cup molasses

Candied fruit (if desired)

2 tablespoons lemon juice

Grind venison and suet. Add all other ingredients except lemon juice in large pot. Simmer 1½ hours or until thick. Remove from heat and add lemon juice. Put in jars and seal. Makes 3 to 4 quarts. I think a Crock-Pot would be great to cook this.

PANSY BOWEN
Missoula, Montana

BEER-BATTERED, DEEP-FRIED FROG LEGS

8 pairs frog legs

2 eggs, well beaten

⅔ cup beer

1 cup flour

½ teaspoon salt

2 tablespoons vegetable oil

Oil for deep frying

2–3 cloves garlic, crushed

Clean and dry frog legs. Combine eggs and beer, then slowly beat in flour, salt, and 2 tablespoons oil until batter is smooth. This amount of batter will comfortably coat about 8 pairs of frog legs. Heat frying oil to 375°F. Add garlic cloves to oil and remove them when they turn light brown before frying frog legs. (This flavors the oil but keeps the garlic from burning and turning the oil brown.) Dip frog legs in batter until well coated and deep fry in hot oil until golden (about 15 minutes). Drain on paper towels. Serve hot.

MARY ANNE LECCE
Collinsville, Illinois

TANGY BEAR CHOPS

4 bear chops or meat from roast cut ½-inch thick
½ teaspoon salt
⅛ teaspoon pepper
2 medium onions, chopped
2 celery ribs, chopped
1 large green pepper, sliced
1 14½-ounce can stewed tomatoes
½ cup ketchup
2 tablespoons vinegar
2 tablespoons brown sugar
2 tablespoons Worcestershire sauce
1 tablespoon lemon juice
1 beef bouillon cube, crushed
2 tablespoons cornstarch
2 tablespoons water
Hot cooked rice (optional)

Place meat in a slow cooker; sprinkle with salt and pepper. Add the onions, celery, green pepper, and tomatoes. Combine ketchup, vinegar, brown sugar, Worcestershire sauce, lemon juice, and bouillon; pour over meat and vegetables. Cover and cook on low for 5–6 hours.

Mix cornstarch and water until smooth; stir into liquid in slow cooker. Cover and cook on high for 30 minutes or until thickened. Serve over rice if desired. Serves 4 to 6, depending on number of chops or cut roast used.

BARBARA FERRICK
Pagosa Springs, Colorado

BAKED PORK CHOPS

6–8 medium pork chops (boneless are best)

Oil or fat for frying

Salt, pepper, and tenderizer

2 10¾-ounce cans condensed cream of mushroom soup

1 medium onion, sliced into rings

1 medium green pepper, sliced into rings

¾ cup water

Season pork chops with salt, pepper, and tenderizer. Brown pork chops on both sides in hot fat. Place a layer of cream of mushroom soup in the bottom of a large baking dish. Place 3 or 4 pork chops on top of the soup. Add a layer of onion rings, green pepper rings, and another layer of mushroom soup. Repeat a second layer of pork chops, onion rings, green pepper rings, and remaining mushroom soup. Pour water over casserole, cover with aluminum foil, and bake at 350°F for approximately 45 minutes or until hot and bubbly.

RON AND KAY DUNLAP
Onalaska, Washington

BAKED HAM AND BEANS

1 10-pound bone-in shank ham

Whole cloves

4 15½-ounce cans assorted beans (garbanzo, red, black, navy,
    kidney, etc.), drained and rinsed

1 4-ounce can diced fire-roasted green chiles (optional)

1 medium onion, chopped

1 or 2 cloves garlic, chopped

2 tablespoons each honey, molasses, and brown sugar

1 14½-ounce can diced peeled tomatoes

1 teaspoon black pepper

1 teaspoon each basil, oregano, thyme, and chili powder

Pinch of cayenne pepper

Dash each of Worcestershire sauce and red wine vinegar

1 beef bouillon cube dissolved in 1 cup boiling water

Place ham on rack in shallow roasting pan, skin side down. With a sharp knife score top of ham with shallow cuts and place whole cloves in slits. Roast uncovered at 325°F approximately 25 minutes per pound (over 4 hours for a 10-pound ham) until internal temperature reaches at least 160°F on a meat thermometer. When cooked, allow ham to cool on counter top for approximately 1 hour, then refrigerate immediately, wrapped in aluminum foil, for at least 12 hours.

Remove skin and trim outer fat layers from cooked ham. The cooling period will firm up ham for easier slicing and trimming. Cut ham into either ham steaks or thin ham slices. Package in resealable plastic bags and freezer wrap and freeze for later use in camp. Label outside of packages with grease pencil for ease in finding in the cooler while in camp. Save all edible chunks and pieces of ham from the slicing process and trim all fat away.

Place ham bone and remaining chunks and pieces in a deep 4-liter baking dish with lid. Add remaining ingredients except bouillon broth and mix slightly. Cover

mixture with bouillon broth to ¼ to ½ inch below top of baking dish. Cover and bake slowly at 300°F for 2–2½ hours. Remove bone and scrape remaining meat from bone and add to mixture. Stir slightly with slotted spoon. Bake another ½–1 hour until beans absorb most of liquid. Don't overcook, as beans will tend to "mush." Beans will absorb some liquid after cooling. Allow cooling for at least 1 hour before handling.

Package beans in doubled resealable plastic bags and freezer wrap. Label outside of packages with grease pencil. Freeze hard at least 2–3 days before leaving for camp.

BILL ROMPA
Albany, Oregon

Deep-Fried Reptile

Remember that fresh meat is important! Select alligator not more than 6 feet long, kill, skin, and separate tail meat into "fingers" (see next page). Select rattlesnake or copperhead at least 3 feet long, kill, skin, and fillet. Piece of meat to be fried should be not more than 6 inches long, and if alligator, not thicker than two fingers. Rattlesnake will be about like a piece of thin bacon. Either type of meat can be coated in commercial deep-fry coating mix for frying fish or vegetables, or simply rolled in a mixture of flour and black pepper, dipped in milk and egg, and rolled in flour again. After coating, set aside (refrigerate if possible) for 30 minutes. Deep-fry, using tall-sided vessel and vegetable oil at 350°F with thermometer to monitor temperature. Use tongs to carefully place coated pieces of meat into the oil. Meat is done when it floats on the surface. Drain on brown paper before serving. Alligator will turn out like chicken fingers; rattlesnake will turn out like clams. Very good eating!

BEN WOLCOTT
Milton, Florida

Balls!

Real old-time swampers here in the South enjoy rattlesnake and alligator balls, generally served as an appetizer. This is how to proceed:

The reptile should be dead, but as fresh as possible. If alligator, skin the legs, belly, underside of jaw and underside of tail–the back skin is not removed. If rattlesnake, it is best to remove the head (with extreme care!), slit the belly, pull the hide off, and remove the entrails. Alligators that appear to have reached sexual maturity may not be palatable. Rattlesnakes that appear not to have reached sexual maturity are too small to fool with.

If alligator, fillet the tail, separate muscles, and cut the muscles into finger-size pieces. Save these to be deep-fried. Proceed to bone out the legs, brisket, neck, and jaw muscles. Set the meat aside. If rattlesnake, fillet the snake, cutting down each side from head to hips (the hips are where the tail begins, at the anus). This will produce two long strips of white, almost translucent, meat. Set aside.

Using set-aside meat, chop or hash rattlesnake into small bits. Alligator meat is tough enough to run through a meat grinder if you have one, instead of chopping by hand. Rattlesnake meat is not.

Mix the following ingredients: chopped meat, chopped celery, chopped pepper, chopped onion, cracker crumbs, and egg. Add seasonings such as garlic, salt, and red and black pepper to taste. Use suitable proportions so that the mixture will bind and can be formed with a spoon into fairly stiff balls.

Deep-fry. I suggest using a tall-sided vessel, such as a Dutch oven with at least 2 inches vegetable oil (peanut oil preferred) heated to 350°F (use a deep-fry thermometer to monitor temperature). Use a tablespoon to form the balls and place carefully into the hot oil. When the balls float to the surface and are golden brown, they are done (usually 1–2 minutes). Drain on brown paper before serving. You can practice by making hush puppies first.

Obviously, this recipe has nothing to do with male organs. Any meat will do. You can make cow balls if you want. My experience is that there are never enough balls to satisfy everyone, so be prepared to serve something else pretty quick, maybe the fried alligator on page 147.

BEN WOLCOTT
Milton, Florida

Dry Aging and Slow Defrosting: Maximizing Your Wild Meat's Potential

BY JOHN McGANNON

I can't begin to tell you how many people have asked me, "How do I get rid of that gamey taste in my ducks, geese, venison, elk, caribou, moose, boar, etc.? And why does it always comes out tough?" Well, I can address both issues at one time.

Most wild birds and big game animals are the equivalent of Olympic athletes. They fly thousands of miles during migration or run up and down 10,000-foot mountains for a living. Mature game animals are usually tremendous physical specimens. The only way to break down the structure of their muscles and make the meat tender, without resorting to meat hammers and artificial tenderizing agents, is to give nature time to do its work (at temperatures that discourage bacterial activity). This process is referred to as dry aging.

The best way to wind up with mild-tasting meat is to get all the blood out while leaving the flavorful cellular juices in. That means giving gravity time to do its work, and taking time when defrosting frozen packages of meat.

Most of us don't have a proper aging facility, so we leave that to the butcher or the outfitter—or just hang our meat at camp and hope it stays at the right temperature long enough to achieve a proper dry age. These situations are often volatile and do not produce the desired results, but we do the best we can.

Most people don't realize that you can reintroduce the dry-aging process even after your meat has been frozen, piece by piece! When it's time to thaw and cook your carefully field-dressed, cut, wrapped, and frozen meat, you can all do very well by exercising some organizational discipline! Because at that point you're entering a little window of peril and opportunity where you can either ruin a great piece of meat, or make it much better. If you're careful and take your time, you can get rid of residual, bad-tasting capillary blood, retain internal, good-tasting cellular juices, and make your meat more tender!

Let's say you've had a great year—you killed a nice buck or bull, not too old, perfect! You've done a good, clean job of field dressing, aging, cutting, wrapping, and freezing your meat. Now it's April and you wake up one morning with the taste of juicy venison on your mind.

Here's how *not* to do it: Stumble down to the freezer and pull out that "buried treasure" strip loin, place it on the kitchen counter, and run off to work. Come home and find your steaks completely defrosted, lying in a pool of liquid.

Not good!

Here's why: Fresh meat contains little molecules of internal moisture enclosed within individual cell walls. Upon freezing, those molecules, being mostly water, expand when they freeze, stretching the cell walls. When you take a piece of meat from, say, a freezer set at 10°F, and place it on a countertop to thaw at 65 degrees, the meat undergoes a relatively rapid 55° temperature change. When those moisture molecules thaw that quickly, they burst the cell walls and seep out of the meat, leaving that large pool of liquid under your thawed package of steaks. Retaining as much of that liquid as possible will give you juicier and more flavorful meat.

Here's the right way: When you experience the desire for some juicy, delicious venison, let that desire build for a while, and start planning ahead. Instead of leaving that frozen block of meat on the counter, place it on a plate and put it in the refrigerator. Leave the wrapper intact. You want to slow the defrosting process down to a minimum. This will allow the meat to retain its natural, internal cellular juices. Completely defrosting a two-to-five-pound package of meat will take about three days.

When the meat is totally thawed out, remove the wrapper. Discard the blood that has accumulated. Blood is responsible for most of the aggressive flavors associated with wild game meats. Dry off the defrosted meat, place it on a rack, uncovered, and put it back in the refrigerator. Set a container underneath the rack to catch the blood that will continue to drain from the meat. Arrange the meat so the pieces don't touch, and make sure there is plenty of room under the rack so the meat isn't sitting in the blood. Make sure there is good air circulation around the meat. Now relax a while. You still have a few days to plan your meal and build an appetite for that precious wild meat!

The time needed to properly age your meat will vary, depending on the age of the animal, the condition of the meat before it went into the freezer, how long it was aged originally, and the size of each piece of meat. On average, it will take three to five days to complete the aging process *after the meat has defrosted*. Yes, you'll have to plan ahead at least a week. That's why I said *organizational discipline*.

You can tell if your meat is aged enough by squeezing it with your fingers. If the meat yields slightly to the pressure, it is ready. If it feels rubbery and bounces back, it might need a little longer. When it's ready trim off any excessively dark meat. Cut your meat into steaks across the grain. (I recommend that wild game steaks be cut no thicker than 1–1½ inches. Larger cuts are exposed to heat for too long and therefore have a tendency to lose a good amount of their limited natural juices.) Cook tender cuts of meat—loins, racks, and certain cuts from the upper leg—as hot and fast as possible.

Dry aging and slow defrosting, although time consuming, will give you results you never thought possible. You've worked very hard for your meat, so enjoy it to its maximum potential. I can't tell you how many dinner guests of mine were amazed at the tender, subtle flavors of my wild game meals. Your guests will be just as amazed.

John McGannon, founder and CEO of Wildeats Enterprises, is an eight-year member and current chairman of RMEF's Golden Gate chapter in San Francisco, California. His culinary products and publications have been featured at RMEF's national conventions since 1995. A New York native and graduate of the Culinary Institute of America in Hyde Park, New York, John has worked at some of the finest restaurants in New York, Florida, Los Angeles, San Francisco, Alaska, and Hong Kong. This article is a small sampling of Chef McGannon's next book on maximizing the potential of wild big game. His first book, Outdoor Cuisine, Behind The Scene, *is based on an Outdoor Life Network TV program called* Outdoor Cuisine, *which John hosted. The show featured wild game and fish cooking in rustic settings, emphasizing nutritional awareness and appreciation for the bounty of nature. To learn more, visit www.wildeats.com.*

FOWL

A. J.'S SAUCED GOOSE

1–2 wild geese
2–3 onions
2–3 apples
2–3 potatoes
1 bunch celery with leaves

1 pound mushrooms
1 tablespoon seasoned salt
1 tablespoon salt
1 tablespoon pepper
4 slices bacon for each goose

Preheat oven to 325°F. Place geese into large roaster or disposable aluminum pan. Slice all veggies and apples lengthwise into eighths. Pack goose cavities with the veggies, and put the rest around the geese. Season with salts and pepper. Lay the bacon strips across the top of each goose.

Take half of A. J.'s Cloud Peak Wild Meat Sauce and pour over the top. Top off by putting some chopped celery over the top. Cover and place in oven; check it in 1 hour. Baste with sauce, and continue basting every 30 minutes until done. When nice and brown, cut into the breast to check for doneness. Take from pan and remove the skin and discard. Keep the veggies hot while you carve the birds. Serve with thick slices of homemade bread and butter. You might like to try it with lingonberries.

A. J.'S CLOUD PEAK WILD MEAT SAUCE

½ cup butter
¼ cup Worcestershire sauce
¼ cup soy sauce
1 12-ounce can frozen orange juice
2 cups brown sugar
1 tablespoon salt
1 tablespoon pepper
1 tablespoon seasoned salt
1 tablespoon Accent seasoning

In a medium-size saucepan melt butter and add other ingredients. Simmer over medium heat for 5 minutes, stirring continually. Remove from heat and set aside.

This sauce is great with goose, moose, wild boar ham, ram, and all venison. I have multiplied this recipe by five to serve over 200 people.

A. J. CHRISTIANSEN
Kimball, Nebraska

DAMN GOOD GOOSE

2 goose breasts (if using only one breast, cut marinade in half)
1½ cups soy sauce
1 can of cola
½ cup olive oil
Minced garlic to taste
Salt and pepper to taste
Horseradish to taste (I like wasabi paste)

Make a marinade of soy sauce, cola, olive oil, garlic, salt, pepper, and horseradish. Leave the goose breasts in the marinade overnight.

Preheat oven to 450°F. Sear both sides of meat on a HOT grill for 2–3 minutes and remove. Wrap meat in heavy tinfoil; include some marinade. Make sure meat is completely sealed in foil; this will help keep meat moist. Bake for 30 minutes. Check the meat; you want it medium rare. If the meat isn't quite done, seal up the foil and let the meat sit for another 10 minutes but not in the oven! If this is overdone it will be very dry, as game meat doesn't have much fat to keep it moist. Serves 2 to 3.

J. MATT TAGG
Nibley, Utah

BAKED GOOSE IN A BAG

1 goose

2 cans mushroom soup

1 cup chopped carrots

3 teaspoons sage (fresh is better)

2 cups chopped onions

5 large cloves garlic, smashed

1 teaspoon seasoned salt (I use Johnny's Seasoning)

1 cup chopped celery

2 cups sweet cream sherry

½ teaspoon garlic pepper

8–10 medium red russet potatoes (optional)

1½ cups sliced or whole mushrooms

¾ cup sour cream

½ cup sherry (optional)

Thaw bird completely if frozen and soak in cold water for 12–24 hours. Preheat oven to 500°F. Remove all water/moisture from inside and outside the bird (pat bird dry with paper towels). Season bird inside and out with garlic pepper or other favorite seasonings. Place bird in a roasting pan on a wire rack to keep bird out of the grease. Place in the preheated oven and cook for 20–25 minutes. This sears the bird to keep it moist during the regular baking time and gets rid of most of the grease. Very important!

Remove bird and dispose of grease. Lower oven temperature to 325°F. In a large turkey roasting bag, place the bird, breast down and add the next 10 ingredients. Seal bag with band/tie, place it in the roasting pan, and put in oven to cook for 75 minutes at 325°F.

Remove from oven and add the sliced or whole mushrooms, sour cream, and optional ½ cup of sherry (if you're brave). Seal bag and place back in oven for another 20 minutes (35 minutes if you added the potatoes) at 300°F.

Remove from oven and place bird on carving plate. Let cool for 5 minutes and then carve. In the meantime place all the sauce/gravy and vegetables from the bag in a large serving bowl. After carving individual servings of goose and placing the meat on the plates, generously spoon on the sauce/gravy with vegetables on each plate. The goose should not only be moist and tender but also have a slightly sweet aromatic flavor. Enjoy! You know what to do next!

JAMES PINCH
Spokane, Washington

SHREDDED BARBECUE GOOSE

2 geese, quartered

2 stalks celery, chopped in large pieces

2 carrots, chopped in large pieces

2 large onions, quartered

2 tablespoons chopped garlic

1 tablespoon seasoned salt

2 bottles beer

2 cups barbecue sauce

Additional barbecue sauce

Place first eight ingredients in a large Crock-Pot or slow cooker and let cook for 12–18 hours. Remove meat from pot. Discard remaining ingredients and juice. Remove goose from bones and shred. Meat should pull apart easily. Return shredded meat to pot. Add additional barbecue sauce (as much as desired). Simmer for a couple more hours. Serve on buns.

MARY ANNE LECCE
Collinsville, Illinois

DOVE JALAPEÑO

8 doves
Bottled Italian dressing
Sliced jalapeños (hot or mild, depending on your taste)
Parmesan cheese, sliced
8 strips bacon
Seasoning (onion powder, garlic powder, lemon and pepper seasoning)

Fillet breasts off the bone so you have two halves per breast. Marinade breast meat in Italian dressing for 24 hours (more or less). Remove meat from marinade (save marinade for basting). Place a slice of jalapeño and a slice of Parmesan cheese between breast halves. Wrap in bacon strip, completely encasing the breast halves in bacon. This keeps the breast meat from drying out, plus it adds flavor. Use toothpicks to keep halves together and bacon in place.

Season breast (to taste) before placing on grill. Cook slowly for 15 minutes per side, basting occasionally with remaining marinade. The key is to cook them slowly, either off to the side of the flame, or with grill at highest position. Lower grill and cook directly over flame for approximately 5 minutes per side to brown the bacon. (The cheese will, for the most part, melt out of the halves but it helps to keep them moist and certainly adds flavor.) Serve over rice. Serves 2 to 4.

MIKE SCHWIEBERT
Atascadero, California

DEBBIE ROSSOW'S GRILLED DOVE

12–24 dove breasts (with or without breast plate)

Ground black pepper to taste

1–2 pounds thin-sliced bacon

2–4 green peppers

2–4 red peppers

1–3 banana peppers

2–4 jalapeño peppers

1–3 cayenne peppers

1 onion

2–3 garlic cloves

Clean dove breasts thoroughly under running cold water, place in bowl of salted water, and let stand for 15–20 minutes. Then remove from bowl, sprinkle with pepper, and place in a resealable plastic bag. Put in the refrigerator overnight or while you are preparing the peppers.

In a food processor mince up all peppers, onion, and garlic together: add ground black pepper to taste. Let stand for 15 minutes. When ready to prepare for grill, prepare shallow baking pan large enough to hold all breasts on skewers. Spray pan with cooking spray so that meat will not stick while cooking. Place each dove breast meat side down on 2 strips of crisscross bacon, put a teaspoon of minced peppers in the center, and wrap in the bacon strips over the peppers. Use skewers to secure everything in place. When all dove breasts are wrapped and skewered, place on a preheated barbecue rack 8–10 inches form coals. Cook for approximately 45–60 minutes. When done, the bacon should be crispy.

HEATHER HARROD
Kentucky

SWEET PHEASANT/GROUSE

2–3 pheasant or grouse
Olive or other cooking oil
5–7 large garlic cloves, minced or crushed
3–4 large sweet onions, chopped
2 cups cream sherry
2 cups flour
Garlic pepper, salt, and pepper to taste
Fresh parsley or chopped green onion

Remove the bones from the birds. Place birds in a pan of water to soak while preparing other ingredients. In a large frying pan, add olive oil and garlic and sauté for 3 minutes, and then add the chopped onion and 1–1½ cups of cream sherry. Season to taste. Cook over medium heat until onions are a golden brown (5–8 minutes) and most of the cream sherry has evaporated. Remove onions and place in a baking or casserole pan. Keep onions warm.

Remove pheasant or grouse pieces from water and dredge in flour seasoned in your favorite seasonings. Place the well-floured pieces in the same frying pan (add more olive oil or cooking oil) and fry to a golden brown on both sides. (If you really like garlic, crush a couple of extra cloves and add.)

Now add the balance of the cream sherry to the onions. Carefully remove the pheasant or grouse pieces after frying and place on top of the onions in the baking or casserole pan. Place the pan into a preheated 325°F oven and bake for 45 minutes with the lid on. Remove from oven and take off the lid. Heat oven to 425°F and place pan back in the oven for 10–15 minutes. Cook until there is a slight crispy brown color to all ingredients.

Garnish with fresh parsley or chopped green onion.

JAMES PINCH
Spokane, Washington

BEER DOVE (OR PHEASANT) BREASTS

1 medium onion, chopped (about ½ cup)

2 tablespoons butter

1 10-ounce can tomato soup

⅔ cup beer

1 teaspoon curry powder

½ teaspoon dried oregano, crumbled

Dash pepper

12 dove breasts (or 4 pheasant or chicken breasts)

¼ cup grated Parmesan cheese

In a saucepan cook onion in butter until tender but not brown. Stir in tomato soup, beer, curry powder, oregano, and pepper. Simmer uncovered for 10 minutes. Arrange meat in baking dish. Pour mixture over meat and bake uncovered at 350°F for 50–55 minutes. Sprinkle with grated cheese. Serve with rice. Serves 2 to 3.

MARY ANNE LECCE
Collinsville, Illinois

DOVE BREAST PIQUANT

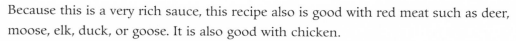

12 dove breasts (or 1½ pounds red meat, such as moose, elk, or deer)
2 cups dry red wine
½ cup olive oil
½ cup soy sauce
¼ cup firmly packed light brown sugar
2 teaspoons ground ginger
1 teaspoon dried oregano, crumbled
1 garlic clove, minced
8 ounces sliced fresh mushrooms

Because this is a very rich sauce, this recipe also is good with red meat such as deer, moose, elk, duck, or goose. It is also good with chicken.

Arrange dove breasts in a large, shallow, nonaluminum baking dish. Mix remaining ingredients in a large bowl. Pour marinade over meat. Cover and refrigerate for at least 2 hours (I usually leave overnight).

Preheat oven to 350°F. Transfer meat and marinade to a large ovenproof skillet. (If using red meat, remove meat from marinade and brown in 2 tablespoons olive oil before proceeding.) Bake uncovered in marinade, basting twice with marinade, for about 40 minutes. Transfer skillet to stove top. Add mushrooms and simmer for 15–20 minutes over medium heat. If desired, thicken sauce with a mixture of flour and water. Serve over rice or noodles. Serves 2 to 3.

MARY ANNE LECCE
Collinsville, Illinois

MARINATED PHEASANT KABOBS

2 boned pheasants, diced into 1-inch pieces

½ pound bacon slices, cut into 2-inch-long pieces

Seasoned salt to taste

Pepper to taste

1 10-ounce can large pineapple chunks

1 red onion, sliced into 1-inch pieces

2 large bell peppers, sliced into 1-inch pieces

20 whole mushrooms, rinsed

5 cloves garlic, chopped

1 teaspoon grated fresh ginger

¼ cup butter or margarine

½ cup brown sugar

4 tablespoons white wine vinegar

4 tablespoons sesame seeds

Wrap each piece of pheasant with a piece of bacon. Season to taste with pepper and seasoned salt. Place meat on skewers alternating with pineapple chunks, onions, bell peppers, and mushrooms. Prepare grill.

Sauté garlic and ginger in butter on low heat. Add brown sugar and vinegar. Cook until smooth. Arrange kabobs on the grill. Baste the kabobs with the sauce while grilling. When done, pour leftover mixture on top of kabobs. Sprinkle with sesame seeds and serve.

JIM WEBER
Helena, Montana

CAPTAIN'S COUNTRY DOVE (OR PHEASANT) BREASTS

2 tablespoons flour

½ teaspoon salt

⅛ teaspoon pepper

12 dove breasts (or 4 pheasant or chicken breasts)

2 tablespoons butter

¼ cup chopped onion

¼ cup chopped green pepper

1 clove garlic, minced

1 teaspoon curry powder

½ teaspoon salt

¼ teaspoon thyme

1 14½-ounce can stewed tomatoes, chopped

2 tablespoons seedless raisins

Combine flour, salt, and pepper in a bag. Add doves (or pheasants) and toss to coat. Melt butter in a skillet. Add floured meat and brown on all sides. Remove meat. Add onion, green pepper, garlic, curry powder, salt, and thyme to the pan and sauté until vegetables are tender. Add tomatoes and simmer, uncovered, for 10 minutes. Add meat and raisins. Simmer, covered, for about 40 minutes or until meat is tender. Serve with rice. Serves 2 to 3.

MARY ANNE LECCE
Collinsville, Illinois

SWEET AND SOUR GRILLED QUAIL (OR DOVE) BREAST

4 whole quail breasts, boned
Seasonings
1 fresh peach, sliced
4 slices bacon
White Wine Baste (recipe follows)
Sweet and Sour Peach Glaze (optional; recipe follows)

Season birds (I use a combination of seasoned salt, seasoned pepper, garlic powder and a barbecue spice blend). Place fresh peach slice in each cavity. Wrap a slice of uncooked bacon around each breast and secure with a toothpick. Grill birds over an indirect heat, basting with White Wine Baste to keep moist. About 5–10 minutes before birds are done, begin glazing them with Sweet and Sour Peach Glaze. Brush glaze on a couple of times, turning birds between applications.

WHITE WINE BASTE

1 cup water
½ teaspoon ground ginger
½ teaspoon garlic powder
1 cup dry white wine

Simmer water with ground ginger and garlic powder to dissolve spices. Add white wine. Stir to blend.

SWEET AND SOUR PEACH GLAZE

1 10-ounce jar peach preserves

¼ cup red wine vinegar

3–4 cloves garlic, minced

1 teaspoon ground ginger

Optional (but very good): Puree a fresh peach (pitted but not peeled) and a fresh jalapeño (seeded) in the food processor and add to the above ingredients. Simmer on stove in saucepan to blend and dissolve.

MARY ANNE LECCE
Collinsville, Illinois

Roast Wild Goose

Salt and pepper inside of goose cavity. Stuff goose with apple, orange, onion, a stalk of celery and a carrot cut in large pieces, as well as 2–3 cloves garlic, smashed. How much you use will depend on the size of the goose. Season outside of goose with salt, pepper, onion powder, and garlic powder.

Place goose in roaster with 3–4 chopped shallots and 1 cup port wine. Roast uncovered at 425°F for 30–45 minutes, until skin is brown. Reduce heat to 350°F. Cover goose and continue roasting for another 2¼–2½ hours, until goose is done. (I usually roast for a total of 3 hours and find that this is sufficient to thoroughly cook the goose.) Add sliced mushrooms to the roaster the last half hour in the oven. Remove goose from roaster. Tent with foil to keep warm.

To make gravy, degrease juices in pan, if needed. Add ½–1 can beef broth (depending on the amount of gravy you want) to juices in pan. Bring to a boil on stove top over medium heat. Thicken with a paste of flour and water, cooking on stove top until thickened. Season with additional salt, pepper, garlic, and onion powder to taste while cooking, if needed.

MARY ANNE LECCE
Collinsville, Illinois

RED RASPBERRY QUAIL

2 cups red wine
2 cups red raspberry syrup
½ teaspoon cayenne pepper
½ teaspoon garlic powder
4 whole quail

Mix first four ingredients and divide in half. In a resealable plastic bag, marinate quail for 8 hours with half of marinade. Grill quail, preferably over indirect heat. Be careful with the heat as the sugar in the marinade will burn if directly over high heat. While quail is grilling, cook other half of marinade until it thickens (you can also use masa or flour to help thicken). Serve sauce over the quail.

PAUL PUNTNEY
Waco, Texas

ARTICHOKE CHICKEN

4 pieces chicken
¾ teaspoon herb pepper
1 6-ounce jar marinated artichoke hearts
1 8-ounce can mushroom pieces, drained and liquid reserved
1 tablespoon flour
¼ cup red wine
1 tablespoon chicken bouillon granules
1 tablespoon fresh parsley

Sprinkle chicken with herb pepper. Brown in 3 tablespoons reserved liquid from artichokes. Push to side and stir in flour and mushroom liquid, wine, bouillon, and a little water if needed. Stir until thickened. Stir in artichoke hearts and mushrooms, cover, and simmer until chicken is tender. Sprinkle with parsley and serve over rice or noodles. Serves 4.

CAROL ALEXANDER
Montrose, Colorado

ROAST QUAIL WITH ARTICHOKE HEARTS

8 tiny white onions or shallots

16 baby artichoke hearts, cooked

2 sticks unsalted butter, softened

8 dressed quail

Salt and freshly ground black pepper

1 teaspoon dried tarragon

1 cup dry white wine

4 large slices country bread, lightly grilled

Preheat oven to 450°F. Skin the onions (they must be small enough to fit inside the quail) and parboil until barely tender. Sauté onions lightly in 2 tablespoons of butter and remove them from the pan. Put one artichoke heart (or ½ if they are large) and one small onion in the cavity of each quail. Tie quail legs together, running the string under the tail to bunch the legs close to the body. Rub the quail with about ¼ cup of the softened butter mixed with salt, pepper, and tarragon. Rub some under the breast skin and fasten the neck skin over the back with a toothpick.

Melt the remaining butter in an ovenproof skillet large enough to hold all eight birds. Brown quail on all sides over medium heat (about 5 minutes total). Add the wine and place the uncovered pan in the preheated oven. After 5 minutes baste the birds and roast another 10 minutes. Baste again and scatter the remaining artichoke hearts around the quail. Roast another 5 minutes, or until done. Arrange two birds on each slice of grilled bread and add a spoonful of artichoke hearts. If all the wine has evaporated, deglaze the pan with a bit more wine and pour pan juices over the birds.

EDITH FERRARIO
Central Point, Oregon

FOUR FOWL FARE

½ pound each wild turkey, grouse, duck, goose, or chicken
    (your choice, choose four), boned and diced
Olive oil
½ pound mushrooms, chopped
2 stalks celery, diced
1 bunch green onions, diced
½ red onion, diced
4 cloves garlic, crushed
1 tablespoon crushed red pepper
1 teaspoon curry powder
Salt and pepper
1 can cream of mushroom soup
¼ cup chopped fresh cilantro or parsley for garnish

In frying pan brown diced meat in olive oil. Add vegetables and seasonings and cook until tender over medium heat. Add cream of mushroom soup, reduce heat, and simmer for 15 minutes. Serve over rice or buttered noodles. Garnish with parsley or cilantro.

JON LONG
Idaho City, Idaho

BROWN RICE AND SAUSAGE STUFFING

2 boxes Uncle Ben's Long Grain and Wild Rice
½ pound bulk pork sausage (unseasoned)
2 medium onions, chopped
6 tart apples, peeled and finely diced
1 cup chopped celery (with a few leaves)

Prepare rice according to directions on box for firm rice. While rice is cooking, in a heavy skillet cook sausage until browned, stirring occasionally to keep loose. Drain off fat and put sausage in a bowl. Add onion, apple, and celery to skillet and sauté about 5 minutes. Add all this mixture and sausage to the cooked rice.

Season quail, dove, chicken breasts (I skin the breasts), or whatever you choose to use, with salt and pepper to taste. Brown in hot oil and then drain on paper towels. Then cover the bottom of a baking dish with half the rice mixture and place birds on top. I drain the grease and use the brown "bits" on top of the birds. Cover the birds with the remainder of the rice. Now sprinkle rice with 2 cups water (or more). Cover baking dish tightly with foil and bake stuffing and browned fowl for at least 2½ hours in 325°F oven.

ARLENE LECCE
Collinsville, Illinois

Smoke-Curing Meats for Fun and Feast

BY TOM MOYSIS

Most people don't realize how easy it is to smoke wild game, fish, beef, pork, or even poultry. We rely on store-bought smoked foods or a friend to smoke our meat for us. But building your own smokehouse is very simple and inexpensive to do.

I've seen people modify dead refrigerators or chest freezers into smokers, but a common and inexpensive one can be made of plywood. A 64-cubic-foot box is big enough to smoke twenty to fifty pounds of meat at a time.

Purchase three sheets of 4-by-8-foot plywood (thickness isn't a factor). Cut them into 4-by-4-foot halves. You will need at least sixteen 2-by-2-by-48-inch boards for corner bindings and rack supports. Using 1½-inch dry-wall screws (you'll need about a pound), and an electric drill or screw-gun, fasten the box pieces together.

To install and remove the smoking grates, a door needs to be mounted on one end of the box. Turn one of the 4-by-4 sheets of plywood into a door by mounting three corner hinges on one side; a plain hasp allows for easy opening and securing the door at the side.

Cut three or four vent holes of at least 2 inches in diameter around the edges of the box top. This will allow for an even airflow and the percolation of heat/smoke around and up through the smoking racks. Each hole needs its own cover to regulate the heat escape. Squares of wood, cans, or any other item wide enough to cover the holes are sufficient. Secure the covers with one nail or screw at top center over the holes. Tighten the nails or screws enough so friction will hold the covers open or closed. The holes are opened and closed according to the temperature inside the box. Open them to lower the temperature; close to hold the smoke inside and/or raise the temperature. You want to maintain a smoking temperature of 80 to 150°F.

The box should be set 12 to 20 inches off the ground with legs or bricks. I use bricks because they won't burn if my smoking fire gets away from me. On breezy days, the bricks will shelter the smoke-producing coals and wood chips (or whatever material you use to generate the smoke), channeling the smoke upward into the smoke-box around your meat.

Smoking grates can be of numerous fabrications. I prefer to use a panel of stretch-steel, strengthened with a 1-inch angle iron welded around the edges. Oven and refrigerator racks can be modified to work. A heavier steel seems to be a safer bet, as raw meat is heavy.

An electric burner can be used for a heat source. It is safe, convenient, reliable, and more easily temperature-regulated than a fire or charcoal. A metal pan or container to hold wood chips is set directly on the burner. The burner temperature level needs to be set high enough for the presoaked wood chips to smolder.

Mesquite is the most common wood used in meat smoking; hickory and several other woods are also popular. Bags of already chipped woods can be purchased at most stores that offer barbecue equipment. My favorite is apple wood/bark taken from trees in my backyard; the apple adds a gentle, sweet-smoked flavor. Even corncobs can be used. Surprisingly, such an off-the-wall item adds a nice smoked flavor.

Meats can be smoked in chunks, slabs, or slices. The thinner the piece, the quicker and more thorough the smoking will be. Whole birds up to the size of a turkey can be smoked. Whole fish, preferably carp or catfish, can be smoked; besides, carp are plentiful and provide a good starting place to learn how to smoke your meats. Hams, loins, and ribs can also be smoked—use high heat to cook for immediate consumption; or cold-smoke them, after which the meats can be frozen.

For several hours to several days, you will need to closely monitor the smoking process to ensure steady temperature and continuous smoke production. Air temperature and wind are always factors, because good air/smoke circulation is crucial. Keeping the temperature below 150°F is a must; 80 to 120° is ideal.

For more ideas and information, look for books at your favorite local bookstore or library.

Tom Moysis is a "displaced farmer" now working as a sales/parts associate at Mark's Machinery in Yankton, South Dakota. An avid hunter and fishing and bowhunting guide, he enjoys eating the game he harvests. He and his family live in Brandon, South Dakota.

FISH AND SEAFOOD

PARMESAN HALIBUT

Fillets of halibut (6 ounces per
    person)
1 medium onion, diced
1 pint mayonnaise
1 ounce freshly ground Parmesan
    cheese
Garden mint

Combine onion, mayonnaise, and cheese,
and cover halibut with mixture. Lightly
sprinkle mint over top and bake at 350°F for
about 25 minutes.

STEVE PUGH
Vancouver, Washington

MOM'S SALMON PATTIES

2 eggs, separated
1 can salmon
4 tablespoons flour
Salt and pepper to taste

Beat egg whites to peak. Add yolks and combine egg mixture with salmon. Beat together.
Add flour, salt, and pepper and shape into
patties. Cook in nonstick skillet with a little
oil until golden on both sides.

    Optional: Add chopped onions and ½
teaspoon Worcestershire sauce to patty mix.

CAROL ALEXANDER
Montrose, Colorado

PARMESAN SALMON

1 large fillet salmon (or large trout or steelhead)

Butter salt

Hickory salt

Onion salt

Lemon pepper

1 medium onion, diced

1 pint mayonnaise

2 ounces freshly grated Parmesan cheese

Place fish in a large baking dish and sprinkle it very lightly with all three salts and lemon pepper. Place in oven under hot broiler. Broil until fish is lightly browned, then remove from oven. Combine diced onion, mayonnaise, and Parmesan. Spread mixture over fish to a thickness of about 1 inch. Put fish back into oven. Turn oven off, letting the heat from the broiler cook fish for another 20 minutes.

STEVE PUGH
Vancouver, Washington

Firepit Fish

Rub clean fish with liquid margarine. Sprinkle with salt, garlic powder, and lots and lots of dry dill weed. Place on foil made like a pan and place on a grill to cook. Cook fish on both sides.

CAROL ALEXANDER
Montrose, Colorado

GRAVLAX

3–4 pounds fresh salmon (select the middle of a 6–7 pound salmon)
3–4 cups fresh dill springs
⅔ cup salt (coarse sea salt if you can find it)
½ cup sugar
20 white peppercorns, crushed
Pinch of saltpeter (Sorry, fellows!)

Clean salmon and remove all bones; split through the back. Wipe both sides thoroughly with clean cloth. Place some dill on the bottom of a deep glass baking dish, mix salt and pepper and a little saltpeter (to retain the red color of the salmon). Rub the spice mixture into the flesh sides. Place one piece skin side down on top of the dill. Sprinkle with spices and cover it with dill sprigs. Sprinkle some spices on other half. Place with skin side up, so that the flesh sides of both pieces are together. If you have dill left, sprinkle it over the fish. Cover with a board and weigh it down with about 4 pounds. Let set in refrigerator for 10–12 hours. Rotate and place the top piece on the bottom and then put back in the refrigerator, for 10–12 more hours.

Remove pieces from the bowl. Discard dill and wipe off excess spices. Slice some thick pieces and arrange them on a platter. Garnish with fresh dill sprigs. Serve with dressing, poached eggs, buttered spinach, and baby new potatoes.

DRESSING

3 tablespoons olive oil or vegetable oil
1½ teaspoons white vinegar
1 tablespoon French mustard or
    Strong Swedish Mustard
    (see recipe page 195)
¼ tablespoon salt
Dash of white pepper

Stir ingredients until blended. Can be made in advance.

A. J. CHRISTIANSEN
Kimball, Nebraska

SESAME SHRIMP AND ASPARAGUS

1 tablespoon sesame seeds

1½ pounds asparagus, cut into 2-inch pieces

1½ pounds shrimp (large), deveined

2 small green onions, sliced

½ cup vegetable oil

4 teaspoons soy sauce

1¼ teaspoons salt

In a 12-inch skillet over medium heat, toast sesame seeds until golden, stirring and shaking skillet. Transfer seeds to a small bowl. In same skillet over medium-high heat, cook asparagus, shrimp, and onions in hot oil until shrimp are pink and vegetables are tender/crisp, stirring frequently (about 5 minutes). Stir in seeds, soy sauce, and salt until blended. This is a springtime favorite. Our family picks lots of wild asparagus and this is one of our favorite ways to use it. Serves 6.

SUZETTE HORTON
Idaho Falls, Idaho

Baked Fish

First catch your fish, trout, bass, or salmon. Clean fish and dredge it in flour, salt, and pepper. Put a small cinnamon stick inside each fish. Bake at 350°F for about 20 minutes, then turn and bake 20 minutes more. (Bake longer for larger fish.) If you don't have stick cinnamon, sprinkle a little ground cinnamon inside each fish.

STEVEN E. BAILEY
Elizabeth, Colorado

DEVILED CRAB PATTIES

3 8-ounce cans lump crabmeat (best you can buy) or fresh crabmeat
4 hard-boiled eggs, finely chopped
¼ cup finely chopped onion
¼ cup finely chopped celery
Small amount of butter
¼ cup flour
¼ cup butter or margarine
¼ teaspoon salt
⅛ teaspoon pepper
1 cup milk
Accent seasoning to taste
2 eggs
1 cup water
Flour for dredging
Cracker meal for dredging
Crushed bread crumbs for dredging
Oil for frying

Pick through the crabmeat and remove all shell and cartilage. Mix chopped eggs with the crabmeat in a bowl. Sauté onion and celery in a small amount of butter. Add onion and celery to crabmeat and egg mixture and mix well.

Make a white sauce by melting ¼ cup butter or margarine in a small saucepan. Stir in flour, salt, and pepper. Add milk all at once. Cook over low heat, stirring constantly, until thickened and bubbly. Cook, stirring, 1–2 minutes more. Remove from heat and mix with the crabmeat mixture. Add some Accent to bring out the flavor of the crabmeat. Put mixture into a bowl, then cover and chill overnight in the refrigerator.

The next day, shape crab mixture into patties. Mix 2 eggs with the cup of water. Dip patties into flour lightly, then into the egg and water mixture. Then dip the patties into the cracker meal, and again into the egg and water mixture. Last, dip the patties into the bread crumbs. Put patties on a tray lined with waxed paper and refrigerate for 3–4 hours.

Heat oil in a heavy skillet. Fry the crab patties until browned on both sides. Makes 18–20 patties.

RON AND KAY DUNLAP
Onalaska, Washington

ISLAND SEAFOOD SAUCE

1 8-ounce container plain yogurt
½ cup mayonnaise or salad
dressing
2 tablespoons ketchup
1 tablespoon lemon juice
1 tablespoon minced onion
½ teaspoon celery seeds

Mix all ingredients in small bowl until well blended. Serve with crab patties, claws, or baked fish. Makes 1½ cups.

KAY DUNLAP
Onalaska, Washington

FISH ITALIANO

4 tablespoons butter

8 ounces fresh mushrooms, sliced

2 tablespoons lemon juice

4 cloves garlic, mashed

½ teaspoon salt

¼ teaspoon pepper

2 pounds halibut or fresh tuna, cubed

2 teaspoons seasoned salt

2 teaspoons seasoned pepper (such as garlic pepper)

2 teaspoons Italian seasoning blend

¼ cup dry white wine

3 cups diced fresh tomatoes (or 2 15½-ounce cans diced tomatoes)

3 ounces capers, drained

¾ cup grated cheese

1 pound spaghetti, cooked and tossed with a little olive oil

Melt butter in a large sauté pan. Sauté mushrooms, lemon juice, garlic, salt, and pepper, uncovered, over medium-low heat for 5–7 minutes. Add fish, seasoned salt, seasoned pepper, Italian seasoning, and wine. Simmer, uncovered, over medium heat for 10 minutes. Add tomatoes and continue simmering, uncovered, over medium heat for 10 more minutes. Add capers and grated cheese. Stir to blend and cook long enough to just heat through. Serve over spaghetti. Serves 4.

MARY ANNE LECCE
Collinsville, Illinois

Cheap Meat

BY TED KERASOTE

One of the arguments I hear from anti-hunters is that hunting is not cost-effective. As Don Barnes of the National Anti-Vivisection Society once commented, "To go out and hunt, it costs you ten times as much money as it would to go buy flesh from a grocery store." This old saw has been repeated so many times—in print, on TV, and even by hunters—that it has taken on the strength of truth. Indeed, the notion that hunting is an inefficient way to fill the larder has even been given coverage in *Bugle.*

As one writer put it, "[M]ost people cannot truthfully say that elk hunting is an economically efficient means of procuring protein. By the time you figure in the cost of licenses, tags, guns and ammunition or bows and arrows, gas, food, lodging, clothing, and other hunting or camping paraphernalia, the price per pound of elk gets pretty steep. This does not take into consideration the uncertainty involved: You could invest all of this money and still not get an elk. It quickly becomes apparent that if you truly wanted to do things in the most efficient, least risky manner, you would get your protein by buying a side of beef."

This writer went on to say that, given the economic inefficiency of elk hunting, we do it for other reasons—most notably the enjoyment of being connected to nature. On the latter point, I have nothing but agreement. However, I have to disagree that hunting is an expensive and risky way of getting protein.

Let's take the question of expense first. Since I've kept careful records of the animals I've killed, the pounds of meat I've gotten from them, and what I've spent on hunting equipment, coming up with some hard numbers as to the cost-effectiveness of hunting isn't all that hard to do.

From 1985 until the writing of this essay in 2003, I've used one firearm for big game: a Ruger M-77, bolt-action, ultralight .30-06 rifle, with a Leupold 2.5-8 Vari-X III scope. (Before that, I used my boyhood rifle—a little Remington

Mohawk .308 with iron sights—but just being a kid in love with hunting, I kept no records of the costs of what I was doing.) In 1985, when I graduated, so to speak, to a significant elk rifle, the Ruger and its Leupold scope cost $455 and $228, respectively. Since they could be had for slightly less than retail, I'm including in those figures the cost of a leather military sling, scope caps, and a cleaning kit, which I also bought.

In the ensuing years I've shot fifteen elk, eighteen pronghorn antelope, two white-tailed deer, two mule deer, and one caribou with this rifle, using sixty-three cartridges, or an average of 1.66 shots per animal. These sixty-three rounds represent just over three boxes of ammo for eighteen years of hunting. Add a box of cartridges at $20 per box each year for sighting in and practice. My hunting licenses cost about $100 each year, for an elk, deer, and two pronghorn licenses.

When all these numbers are rolled into an amortization calculation, which was done by my CPA and fellow Rocky Mountain Elk Foundation member Randy Newberg of Bozeman, Montana, the cost of my rifle, scope, ammo, and licenses has been $157.11 per year. For the mathematically inclined, this calculation was done as follows: In today's dollars, the cost of my rifle and scope was $1,167.96, figured at a compounded rate of inflation of 3.2 percent per year, the data obtained from the Federal Reserve Bank in Minneapolis. Subtract their used sale price ($500 in the northern Rockies) and divide by 18 years. The result is an amortized cost of $37.11 per year, with $120 added on each year for the ammunition and hunting licenses.

That takes care of the cost of basic tools. Now for what the tools have produced: On average, I get 120 pounds of boneless, packaged meat from an elk and 40 pounds from a pronghorn. I got 105 pounds of meat from the caribou I shot while on a long canoe trip in Alaska, when I was spending a lot of time in the state, 65 pounds from the mule deer buck, 50 pounds from the white-tailed buck, and 40 pounds from each of the two doe deer, for a total of 2,820 pounds of meat.

Now take my hunting cost of $157.11 per year and multiply it by 18 years. The total is $2827.98. If this figure is then divided by 2,820 pounds of meat, the cost to obtain my wild diet is about $1.00 per pound in today's dollars.

Of course, there are those who will point out that I take time out to hunt and that time is money, not to mention that I spend money on clothing and equipment, i.e., paraphernalia. But if other recreators aren't faulted for using their free time to play golf, ski, or watch football, why should a hunter, hunting on weekends, be saddled with the time-is-money argument? The high cost of gear shouldn't be an issue, either. Like many elk hunters, I hunt in the same outdoor clothing I use to backpack or ski—the same pants, long underwear, jackets, boots, and summit pack, throwing an orange vest over my shoulders to make me legal. As for gasoline to drive to and from the roadhead, I would use the same gasoline to take a hike or to ski. Where I live, this is a pretty short distance: about 5 miles. And just so the claim of Rocky Mountain elitism won't be leveled, there are hundreds of thousands of other hunters, in cities all over North America, who can hunt white-tailed deer just as close to their homes as I hunt elk, especially using a bow.

As for the risk of not getting an elk—that's pretty small as well. Virtually everyone I know who puts in a few weekends of elk hunting kills an elk. As a friend of mine likes to say, "Getting an elk each year is the reward of doing what comes natural to anyone who likes being outside." Anyone who walks through country early and late and pays attention is bound to get close to elk. The line of thought that says hunting is difficult may bolster the ego, but, aside from an occasional run of bad luck, it doesn't hold water—particularly if you're looking for edible protein instead of antlers. In many parts of the eastern United States, the same holds true. It's difficult not to get a doe deer if you can shoot a bow with reasonable accuracy. One of the things that makes elk hunting so attractive is that you're rewarded with a lot of meat when you get one.

Now for the interesting part—how does $1.00 per pound for wild meat compare with what that sum will buy in a grocery store? If, as some anti-hunters have pointed out, wild meat is ten times pricier than supermarket meat, beef should cost 10 cents a pound. This is hardly the case. At Wild Oats, a chain store that bills itself as "North America's premier natural foods retailer," Coleman Natural Beef, raised in Saguache County, Colorado, sells for $4.99 a pound for 93 percent lean ground beef, $8.99 for top sirloin, $12.99 for T-bones, and $19.99 for tenderloins. In other words, my wild meat—as natural as natural can be—is 80 percent cheaper than organic beef burger and between a ninth and a twentieth the price of organic beef steak. My elk meat even is cheaper than ordinary beef sold in chain supermarkets, where in 2003 ground beef goes for between $1.49 and $1.99 a pound and tenderloins are $10.99 a pound.

But price isn't the only way to compare wild meat to domestic. Elk, antelope, deer, and moose are free-ranging grazers or browsers. They contain no antibiotics or growth hormones, nor are they "finished"—fed grain—on a feedlot to fatten them. Even Coleman "natural" beef is finished with grain for a week before slaughter. Meat that comes from grass-fed animals is healthier than meat from animals fed grain. It has about 100 fewer calories per 6-ounce serving, one-half to one-third the amount of "bad" saturated fat, and two to six times more "good" fat, called omega-3 fatty acids. Omega-3s are friendly to your heart and blood pressure, and some researchers believe that they lower the risk of cancer. Even an animal that spends only one month on a feedlot eating grain quickly loses about half of the omega-3 fatty acids it has accumulated while eating grass on the open range.

In addition, one would be remiss not to mention that the health benefits of elk hunting—like the warming benefits of cutting firewood—play themselves out more than once. Hiking up mountainsides, field-dressing elk, carrying out quarters, loading panniers, and riding ponies all exercise a hunter's circulatory system more than pushing a shopping cart down an aisle in a supermarket. A complete analysis of the costs of elk hunting would have to include the medical bills a person avoids by hiking the vertical world of elk country.

Last, and certainly not least, eating wild meat is good for the planet. Factory farms, whether growing cattle, hogs, or chickens, concentrate organic wastes and pollute both soil and water. Beef in particular uses enormous amounts of oil in the shape of fertilizer and the fuel to run the farm machinery that plants and harvests corn. In fact, one calculation has shown that it takes roughly 284 gallons of oil to take a beef calf from birth to a 1,250-pound steer. As writer Michael Pollan once observed in a *New York Times Magazine* article about the ecological effects of the cattle industry, "We have succeeded in industrializing the beef calf, transforming what was once a solar-powered ruminant into the very last thing we need: another fossil-fuel machine."

Elk, it hardly bears repeating, are grown by the earth for free.

Of course, how much an individual spends on hunting will vary with how much specialized equipment and clothing he or she buys (one might call this the Cabela's factor), whether the hunter processes the meat or has a butcher do the job, and how far the hunter travels to hunt. Nevertheless, the facts speak for themselves. Hunting elk can be one of the least expensive ways to fill your gut as well as your soul.

Ted Kerasote, veteran carnivore, RMEF Habitat Partner, and frequent contributor to Bugle, *also writes for many other magazines, including* Audubon *and* Outside. *He is the author of several books, including* Bloodties *and* Heart of Home. *He lives in Wyoming.*

MARINADES, SPICES, AND SAUCES

KEN JOSEPH'S WILD GAME MARINADE

⅔ cup vegetable oil

⅓ cup soy sauce

⅛ teaspoon ground ginger

½ onion, minced

¼ teaspoon pepper

¼ teaspoon garlic powder

2 tablespoons white vinegar

2 tablespoons honey

Mix ingredients well and pour over meat. Marinate in refrigerator for 24 hours (a couple of hours will also do the trick if you're in a hurry). Note: We like elk without the honey and deer meat with the honey.

KEVIN AND ANNETTE JOSEPH
Dolores, Colorado

SPICE MIXTURE FOR WILD GAME

9 teaspoons seasoned salt

5 teaspoons seasoned pepper

4 teaspoons barbecue seasoning blend

2 teaspoons garlic powder

1 teaspoon oregano

½ teaspoon cayenne pepper (optional)

Mix ingredients and store in an empty 3-ounce spice jar. Season meat with spice mixture, then marinate in one of the following marinades for at least 1 hour (or overnight). Add meat tenderizer if desired. Baste meat with marinade while cooking to keep moist.

MARY ANNE LECCE
Collinsville, Illinois

MARINADE I

2 tablespoons Worcestershire sauce
4 tablespoons dry sherry
6 tablespoons steak sauce
   (such as A1)
Dash of Tabasco sauce (optional)

Marinate meat for at least 2 hours (or overnight). Grill or broil (grilled is better) until done as desired.

MARY ANNE LECCE
Collinsville, Illinois

MARINADE II

2 tablespoons red wine vinegar
¼ cup Worcestershire sauce
½ cup port wine
⅛ teaspoon cayenne pepper
   (optional)
2 shallots, chopped fine
1 tablespoon chopped garlic
8 ounces fresh sliced mushrooms
1 beef bouillon cube
1 cup water
1 tablespoon cornstarch

Marinate seasoned meat in first six ingredients for at least 2 hours (or overnight). Grill or broil (grilled is better) until done as desired. While meat is cooking, pour remaining marinade in a small saucepan. Add mushrooms, bouillon cube, and water. Simmer over medium heat. Thicken with 1 tablespoon cornstarch mixed with some cold water. Serve as sauce with meat.

MARY ANNE LECCE
Collinsville, Illinois

DEER CAMP BBQ MARINADE AND SAUCE

1 cup molasses

1 cup honey

1½ cups dark brown sugar

1½ cups Worcestershire sauce

1½ cups prepared mustard

1 quart ketchup

½ cup fresh ground pepper

½ cup crushed red pepper flakes

2 quarts red wine vinegar

2 quarts water

1 quart white wine

1½ cups kosher salt

Put all ingredients in a 12-quart kettle and simmer for 30 minutes. Stir occasionally. Cool and store in plastic or glass jugs (doesn't need refrigeration). Use to marinate chicken, chicken wings, pork chops, beef steaks, or game for at least 2 days. Barbecue or broil to taste, basting frequently with leftover marinade. Makes about 1¾ gallons.

TERRY LINDLEY
Bigfork, Montana

CITRUS BALSAMIC GRILL

⅓ cup lemon juice

¼ cup Worcestershire sauce

3 tablespoons balsamic vinegar

1 tablespoon olive oil

2 teaspoons chopped garlic

2–2½ pounds venison, moose, or
    elk steak or chicken parts

Combine marinade ingredients and mix well. Pour mixture over meat or chicken in a nonmetal container. Marinate for 2 hours or overnight. Grill until done as desired, using marinade to baste and keep meat moist.

MARY ANNE LECCE
Collinsville, Illinois

ORIENTAL GRILL

1 cup water

¾ cup soy sauce

⅔ cup dry sherry

½ cup packed dark brown sugar

6 cloves garlic, minced

1 tablespoon ground red (cayenne) pepper

1 tablespoon grated fresh ginger (or 1½ tablespoons ground ginger)

2 teaspoons Chinese five-spice powder

2–2½ pounds venison, moose, or elk steak or chicken parts

Combine marinade ingredients and mix well. Pour mixture over meat or chicken in a nonmetal container. Marinate for 2 hours or overnight. Grill until done as desired, using marinade to baste and keep meat moist.

MARY ANNE LECCE
Collinsville, Illinois

A. J.'s Juniper Seasoning Mix

The Swedish use juniper berries to season moose, roe deer, and other wild things.

To make the seasoning, gather the ripe juniper berries on your fall hunting trips. It takes 2–3 years for the seeds to ripen. They turn dark when ripe.

Dry the berries thoroughly. Do not use air-tight containers; a dehydrator works well. Place dried berries in a plastic bag and crush with a rolling pin. Set aside. Heat 2 tablespoons butter until it is light brown. Add 2 tablespoons flour and stir over low heat for 2–3 minutes. Add a cup of game stock or a crushed bouillon cube in a cup of water and simmer for 15 minutes, stirring now and then. Add ½ cup of home-made chokecherry wine or a substitute; salt and pepper to taste. Add 2 tablespoons of crushed juniper berries and simmer for 10 minutes. If sauce is too thick add stock, a spoonful at a time, until it is the way you like it.

Note: Juniper berries are used in making gin.

A. J. CHRISTIANSEN
Kimball, Nebraska

KILLER FISH/POULTRY MARINADE

½ **cup olive oil**

2 tablespoons chopped garlic (more if desired)

2 tablespoons chopped fresh ginger (more if desired)

½ **tablespoon salt**

1 tablespoon black pepper

**1 tablespoon crushed dried red pepper (use more or less if you like it
    hotter/less hot)**

Mix all ingredients. Marinate raw fish/poultry in a plastic bag for at least 6 hours (preferably 12 hours or more). This is best when meat is cooked on the grill, but the oil in this marinade will flame up on the grill. This is bad; it will give the meat a charred/burned taste. To combat this, put the meat on the grill very fast and put the lid down to smother the flames. A squirt bottle to extinguish the flames will work as well. Put the meat on the HOT grill and sear each side well, then turn down the heat (medium to low heat works well) and cook until done.

When cooking fish it is important to not overcook it. The thickness of the fillets will determine how long to cook it. Fish cooks fairly fast—as a general rule a fillet ½ inch thick will usually be done in about 6 minutes (3 minutes per side)—however, each grill cooks a little differently. Watch it constantly and cook only until it flakes with a fork and is completely opaque.

J. MATT TAGG
Nibley, Utah

CHINESE MUSTARD

1 can beer
1–1½ tablespoons dry mustard
  powder

Stir ½ can of beer and 1 table-spoon dry mustard in sauce bowl. Try 'er out. If it's not hot enough, kick in some more powder. Cinch your sombrero down tight and give 'er a twist! The ½ can you have left should resuscitate you for a little while. Have another handy! And be close to the creek in the morning.

A. J. CHRISTIANSEN
Kimball, Nebraska

STRONG SWEDISH MUSTARD

¼ cup very strong Swedish coffee
  (this will take about a week of
  boiling in the elk camp)
¼ cup pale mustard powder
⅛ teaspoon salt
¼ tablespoon sugar

Mix it up in a bowl and with a spoon that will not melt.

A. J. CHRISTIANSEN
Kimball, Nebraska

HOLLORAN RANCH MARINADE

1 cup soy sauce

1 tablespoon honey

½ cup red wine

1 tablespoon olive oil

2 tablespoons chopped fresh ginger

Combine all ingredients in a saucepan. Heat slightly to dissolve honey. Marinate wild game or even beef for 1–2 hours. Grill to your liking.

CHIP CLEARY
Colorado

ELK MARINADE (FROM MONTANA VOLUNTEER SUMMER RENDEZVOUS 2000)

1½ cups olive oil

¾ cup soy sauce

¼ cup Worcestershire sauce

2 tablespoons dry mustard

2¼ teaspoons salt

1 tablespoon fresh-ground pepper

½ cup red wine vinegar

1½ teaspoons dried parsley flakes

2 crushed garlic cloves

⅓ cup fresh lemon juice

Combine all ingredients and mix well. Marinate meat overnight in stainless steel bowl. Covers approximately 3 pounds of meat.

DAN TROCHTA
West Yellowstone, Montana

TERIYAKI MARINADE AND BASTING SAUCE

Soy sauce
Sugar
Crushed garlic
Ginger
8 ounces tomato sauce
4–6 ounces white wine

Pour soy sauce into saucepan and warm on stove. Add sugar, stirring to dissolve until you get a sweet soy taste—not salty. Add garlic until you get garlicky sweet soy taste. Add ginger a little at a time to taste. Add tomato sauce. Add white wine. Stir to mix and dissolve all sugar. Store in refrigerator. Marinate chicken, pork, and game meat at least 2 days—longer is better. Barbecue or oven roast, basting every 15 minutes with leftover marinade.

TERRY LINDLEY
Bigfork, Montana

COCKTAIL SAUCE

2 cups ketchup
3 tablespoons horseradish
2 tablespoons Worcestershire sauce
Tabasco sauce to taste
1–2 tablespoons cola

Blend and adjust to taste. Use on clam strips, calamari strips, shrimp, and oysters.

TERRY LINDLEY
Bigfork, Montana

DESSERTS

PUMPKIN PIE CAKE

CRUST

1 package yellow cake mix (set aside 1 cup for topping)
¼ cup margarine
1 egg

FILLING

1 can pumpkin (size for 1 pie)

TOPPING

1 cup cake mix
1 teaspoon ground cinnamon
¼ cup sugar
¼ cup chilled margarine

For the crust: Combine the cake mix, margarine, and egg until thoroughly mixed. Press into a 9-by-13-inch pan.

For the filling: Follow directions on the can for making pie filling. Pour on top of crust.

To finish: Mix topping ingredients and sprinkle on top of the filling. Bake at 350°F for 1 hour or until center is set.

PANSY BOWEN
Missoula, Montana

SUGAR BEET CAKE

2 eggs
4 cups grated sugar beets
1¼ cups sugar
2 teaspoons cinnamon
½ cup vegetable oil
1 cup nuts
2 cups flour
1 teaspoon salt
2 teaspoons baking soda

Mix eggs and sugar beets. Add remaining ingredients and mix well. Pour batter into greased 9-by-13-inch pan and bake for 45 minutes at 350°F.

GLAZE

½ cup butter
2 cups brown sugar
½ cup milk

Boil and pour over cake. Decorate with extra nuts.

CAROL ALEXANDER
Montrose, Colorado

KAY'S SOUR CREAM POUND CAKE

4 eggs
1 package yellow butter cake mix
¼ cup sugar
½ cup vegetable oil
¼ cup water
½ pint sour cream

Mix eggs and cake mix; add sugar, oil, and water and beat until smooth. Fold in sour cream and pour mixture into a pound-cake pan. Preheat oven to 375°F and cook for 45 minutes. (Note: I bake my cake at 350°F for 45 minutes. It all depends on how hot your oven gets.)

GLAZE

1 cup sugar
½ cup water
1 teaspoon almond flavoring

Combine all ingredients and boil for 1 minute. Pour over top of cake while both are still warm.

LEMONY HONEY TOPPING

½ cup whipping cream
3 tablespoons honey
1 tablespoon lemon juice
½ teaspoon grated lemon peel

In a small mixing bowl, combine whipping cream, honey, and lemon juice. Beat with an electric mixer on low speed for about 5 minutes or until soft peaks form (tips curl). Gently fold in the lemon peel. Serve immediately or chill for up to 1 hour. Serve over slices of cake or fresh fruit. Makes about 1 cup.

RON AND KAY DUNLAP
Onalaska, Washington

RHUBARB SURPRISE CAKE

3 cups cut-up rhubarb

1½ cups water

1 cup sugar

1 3-ounce package strawberry gelatin

1 white cake mix

2 cups miniature marshmallows

Boil rhubarb, water, and sugar. Remove from heat, add powdered gelatin, and set aside.

Grease 9-by-13-inch cake pan. Cover the bottom with marshmallows. Make cake mix according to package directions. Pour cake batter on the marshmallows, pour rhubarb mixture over all. Bake according to cake mix directions.

LARRY WINNER
Boise, Idaho

No-Cook Cheesecake

Take a box of graham crackers and crunch them up into the bottom of an 18-by-24-inch pan. Melt 2 sticks of butter and evenly pour this over the crumbs. Take 3 sticks of Philadelphia cream cheese, 1 can Eagle-brand condensed milk, and ½ teaspoon cinnamon. Mix thoroughly. Spread this over the crumbs. Cut up 3 pints of strawberries and gently mix in ½ cup sugar. Pour berries over the mixture in the pie pan. Mix 1 can of ginger ale with 2 packets of unflavored gelatin. Pour this over the strawberries. Refrigerate. It takes about a half hour for the cheesecake to set up. Serve with a dollop of whipped cream or yogurt.

RON SAVAGE
Eugene, Oregon

PEANUT BUTTER CAKE

½ cup vegetable oil
1½ sticks butter
½ cup peanut butter
1 cup water
2 cups flour
1 teaspoon baking soda
2 cups sugar
½ teaspoon salt
1 teaspoon vanilla
2 eggs
½ cup milk

Bring to a boil the oil, butter, peanut butter, and water. Combine the dry ingredients in a bowl. Pour peanut butter mixture over the dry ingredients and mix well. Add vanilla, eggs, and milk. Combine thoroughly. Pour batter into a 10-by-16-inch pan. Bake at 350°F for about 18 minutes.

PEANUT BUTTER ICING

1 stick butter
⅓ cup milk
½ cup peanut butter
1 teaspoon vanilla
1 pound powdered sugar

Heat butter, milk, and peanut butter to boiling point. Add vanilla and powdered sugar. Stir well to combine thoroughly. Ice cake while still warm.

PHYLLIS FUNKHOUSER
Paris, Illinois

MAM-MAW'S BLUE RIBBON POTATO CHIP COOKIES

2 sticks margarine or butter (softened)
⅔ cup sugar
½ cup chopped pecans
2 cups flour
½ cup crushed potato chips
1 teaspoon vanilla

My mother, Mary Alice Pirtle, made these cookies as long as I remember. I've been making them for many years also, and except for one lady (who happens to work for the RMEF in Missoula), I've never met anyone who had heard of or tasted them! They are easy and wonderful!

Mix ingredients with hands until you can form dough into balls about the size of a walnut. Press flat on cookie sheet and bake at 350°F for 15–18 minutes (depending on your oven).

These cookies will not spread, and when done, will be a beige color on top, and a light golden color on the bottom.

CHARLIE PIRTLE
Las Cruces, New Mexico

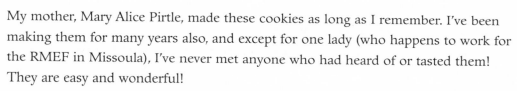

PUMPKIN-APPLE STREUSEL CAKE

APPLES

3 tablespoons unsalted butter

4 cups Granny Smith apples, diced, peeled, and cored

3 tablespoons sugar

1 teaspoon ground cinnamon

CAKE

1½ cups all-purpose flour

1 cup firmly packed golden brown sugar

½ cup (1 stick) unsalted butter at room temperature, cut into pieces

½ teaspoon salt

¾ cup canned puree of pumpkin

⅓ cup sour cream

2 tablespoons sugar

2 teaspoons pumpkin pie spice

1 teaspoon baking soda

2 large eggs

For apples: Melt butter in large nonstick skillet over medium-high heat. Add apples and sauté until apples begin to brown, about 5 minutes. Add sugar and cinnamon and sauté until golden brown, about 3 minutes longer. Let cool.

For cake: Preheat over to 350°F. Butter a 9-inch springform pan. Combine flour, brown sugar, butter, and salt in a large bowl. Using an electric mixer, beat until mixture resembles coarse meal. Set aside ⅔ cup of mixture for topping. Beat pumpkin, sour cream, 2 tablespoons sugar, spice, and baking soda into remaining flour mixture, beating just until smooth. Beat in eggs. Transfer batter to the springform pan. Scatter apples evenly over top. Sprinkle reserved topping over apples. Bake cake until

topping is golden brown and tester inserted into center comes out clean, about 1 hour 10 minutes. Cook cake in pan on a wire rack for 20 minutes. Run knife around pan sides to loosen cake. Release pan sides from cake. Transfer cake to platter. Can be made 6 hours ahead. Let stand at room temperature. Serve warm or at room temperature with ice cream. Serves 8.

EDITH FERRARIO
Central Point, Oregon

FRUIT SQUARES

> **2 eggs**
> **½ cup honey**
> **⅔ cup flour**
> **1 cup chopped pecans**
> **1 cup chopped dried fruit (i.e., dried apricots, apples, pineapples, cranberries, or raisins)**
> **½ cup chocolate chips (optional)**

Mix the eggs and honey. Add flour and mix. Blend in the nuts, fruit, and chocolate chips. Scrape into an oiled 8-by-8-inch pan. Bake at 350°F for 30 minutes or until the top begins to brown. Let stand until cool then cut into squares and store in baggies or any tight container.

We use these for hunting camp, pack trips into the wilderness, and river trips because they don't crumble and are always popular. They travel best in an empty Pringle's potato chip container.

JIM FICKE
Steamboat Springs, Colorado

PEANUT BUTTER FINGERS

½ cup butter, softened

½ cup white sugar

½ cup brown sugar

1 egg

½ cup peanut butter

½ teaspoon baking soda

¼ teaspoon salt

½ teaspoon vanilla

1 cup flour

1 cup oats

1 6-ounce package chocolate chips

½ cup powdered sugar

¼ cup peanut butter

2–4 tablespoons canned evaporated milk

Cream butter and white and brown sugar. Add egg, ½ cup peanut butter, baking soda, salt, and vanilla. Blend all together. Stir in flour and oats. Spread in greased 9-by-13-inch pan. Bake at 350°F for 18–20 minutes. When done, sprinkle with chocolate chips. Let stand for 5 minutes.

Combine powdered sugar, ¼ cup peanut butter, and canned milk. Mix well. Spread chocolate chips evenly and then drizzle this peanut butter mixture on top and spread it around.

Delicious even warm!

DWEE MURRAY
Oakville, Washington

SWEDISH APPLE DUMPLINGS

Prepared pie crust
10–12 medium-size sour apples
1 bag slivered almonds
1 cup sugar
¼ cup butter, softened
2 tablespoons ground cinnamon
1 egg, beaten

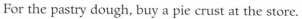

For the pastry dough, buy a pie crust at the store.

Peel and core the apples. Cut the pie crust into squares large enough to fold up over the top of apples. Place an apple in the center of each square. Mix almonds, sugar, butter, and cinnamon and fill apples. Fold the corners of the dough up over the top of each apple and pinch together. Place on a greased baking pan, brush with beaten egg, and sprinkle with sugar, cinnamon, and almond slivers.

Bake in preheated oven at 425°F for 5 minutes, then reduce heat to 350°F and bake until light brown. Serve with Swedish Vanilla Sauce. Serve either hot or cold.

SWEDISH VANILLA SAUCE (VANILJSAS)

3 egg yolks
2 tablespoons sugar
1 cup cream, heated
2 tablespoons vanilla extract
1¾ cups whipped cream

Beat egg yolks and sugar in top of a double boiler. Add heated cream and simmer until thick, stirring constantly. Remove from heat, add vanilla, and cool, beating occasionally. When cold, fold in whipped cream carefully and serve.

A. J. CHRISTIANSEN
Kimball, Nebraska

FLAT APPLE PIE

CRUST

3 cups flour

1 teaspoon salt

½ teaspoon baking soda

1¼ cups shortening

1 egg

6 tablespoons water

1 tablespoon cider vinegar

FILLING

Corn flakes

8 apples, peeled and cut up

1 cup sugar

Ground cinnamon

2 teaspoons butter

For the crust: Combine flour, salt, and baking soda. Cut in shortening. In a separate bowl combine egg, water, and cider vinegar. Stir well. Then add to the pastry mixture with a fork. Now roll out the pastry and cover a 9-by-13-inch baking pan or an 11-by-15-inch baking pan.

For the filling: Lay the corn flakes over the pie crust to cover the bottom. Add a layer of cut-up apples. Sprinkle on the cup of sugar, and sprinkle that with cinnamon. Top with slivers of butter. Now top with the remaining piece of pastry. Seal edges. Slit the top and bake at 350°F for 40 minutes.

ICING

2 cups powdered sugar

1 teaspoon vanilla

3 tablespoons milk

Combine powdered sugar, vanilla, and milk. Beat until smooth. When the pie comes out of the oven, drizzle it with the icing. Eat pie warm with a tall glass of milk or a scoop of ice cream on the side.

DWEE MURRAY
Oakville, Washington

EGGNOG PIE

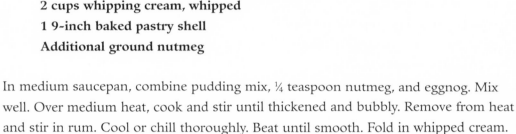

1 6-serving package vanilla flavor pudding mix (not instant)
¼ teaspoon ground nutmeg
1½ cups eggnog
2 tablespoons light rum (or 1 teaspoon rum extract)
2 cups whipping cream, whipped
1 9-inch baked pastry shell
Additional ground nutmeg

In medium saucepan, combine pudding mix, ¼ teaspoon nutmeg, and eggnog. Mix well. Over medium heat, cook and stir until thickened and bubbly. Remove from heat and stir in rum. Cool or chill thoroughly. Beat until smooth. Fold in whipped cream. Spoon into prepared pastry shell. Garnish with additional nutmeg. Chill for 4 hours or until set. Note: When I serve it I sometimes put a dollop of additional whipped cream on the top of each piece and then some nutmeg on that.

MARY ANNE LECCE
Collinsville, Illinois

A. J.'S GARDEN GREEN TOMATO PIE

5 cups sliced green tomatoes
¼ cup salt
5 cups water
1½ cups sugar
3 tablespoons flour
2 tablespoons cornstarch
1 teaspoon ground cinnamon
2 tablespoons bottled lemon juice
2 10-inch pie crusts
1 egg, beaten
(Reduce ingredients by 20 percent for a 9-inch pie)

Soak green tomato slices in salt water (dissolve ¼ cup salt in 5 cups water) for 30 minutes. Drain and dice. Mix the sugar, flour, cornstarch, and cinnamon. Add lemon juice and diced green tomatoes. Stir well. Sprinkle a little flour on bottom crust, and pour in the pie filling mix. Place the top crust on top. Stick your thumb into the middle to vent. Fold the edge and pinch the two crusts together. Brush the top with the beaten egg. Sprinkle with a little sugar and cinnamon. This gives a caramelized coating to the pie. Take fork and poke around on the top.

Preheat oven to 400°F. Bake pie for 15 minutes. Reduce heat to 350°F and bake for 40 minutes until nice and brown. It will bubble up when done.

A. J. CHRISTIANSEN
Kimball, Nebraska

APPLE CRUMB PIE

6–7 medium Granny Smith apples
1 9-inch pie crust (unbaked)
1 cup sugar
½ cup flour
1 cup graham cracker crumbs
⅔ cup chopped walnuts
½ teaspoon ground cinnamon
½ cup butter

Peel apples and cut into wedges (about eight wedges per apple). Arrange apples in a 9-inch unbaked pie crust. In a bowl combine the sugar, flour, graham cracker crumbs, walnuts, and cinnamon. Sprinkle the mixture over the apples in the pie shell. Melt the ½ cup of butter and pour over the apples. Place in a preheated 350°F oven and bake about 45–50 minutes (or until the apples are soft).

Cool for 15–20 minutes. Great with ice cream or whipping cream.

JAMES PINCH
Spokane, Washington

BILL'S ALL-AMERICAN ELK AND DEER CAMP APPLE PIE

FILLING

9 cups sliced apples

½ cup sugar

½ cup packed brown sugar

1 teaspoon ground cinnamon

¼ teaspoon grated nutmeg

1 teaspoon vanilla

¼ teaspoon salt

2 tablespoons lemon juice

CRUST

2 9-inch pie crusts

3 tablespoons all-purpose flour

1 tablespoon (approximately 3 slivers) butter or margarine

Using a slotted spoon, stir together the pie filling ingredients in a 10-cup plastic bowl with an airtight lid. Quarter, core, peel, and thinly slice the apples into the bowl with a small paring knife. As you slice, stir the filling every 2–3 apples to keep the apples from turning brown. The apples will start "juicing" immediately. Mix well before closing lid. Let the filling sit at room temperature for at least 8 hours overnight; 12 hours is better to soften and flavor the apples. Start the filling the night before after dinner and the pie will be ready to bake in the morning.

When ready to bake, preheat the oven to 425°F. Add the filling to the pie crust. Follow the directions on the pie crust box for stuffing the pie. Make sure the pie crust is at room temperature for ease in handling the dough without cracking. Spread

the pie crust on a cutting board lightly sprinkled with flour, and fix any holes or cracks in the crust after unfolded by wetting fingers with water and pressing dough together. Lightly press the crust floured side down into a metal pie tin or cake pan large enough to fit the 9-inch crust. (Metal pie pans will not break in transport or in camp if dropped or knocked around.)

Using a slotted spoon, scoop the apples from the filling mixture leaving the juices behind. Spread the apples evenly in the open crust. Add 3 tablespoons flour to the remaining juices in the bowl and whisk into mixture until the flour is completely absorbed. Pour the floured juice evenly over the apples in the open crust. Top the filling with 3 thin slices of butter or margarine. Close up the pie by placing the 9-inch top crust over the pie and seal the edges of the pie with your fingers to press the top and bottom crusts together. Lightly sprinkle the top crust with sugar and cut 3 or 4 small slots into the top crust to allow steam to escape while the pie is baking. Cover the outside edges of the pie with 2-inch strips of aluminum foil to keep from burning the crust edges for the first hour of baking. Place a cookie pan on the bottom rack of oven to catch any drippings during baking. Cover the cookie sheet with aluminum foil to ease in cleaning up.

Place pie on next rack above cookie sheet and bake at 425°F for the first 15 minutes. Lower oven temperature to 350°F and bake for another 60 minutes. Remove aluminum foil from crust edges without removing pie from oven by sliding out rack and complete final baking and browning for another 15 minutes. Then remove pie from oven and place on a cooling rack so air can completely surround and cool pie.

Note: This recipe will make one 9-inch pie, enough to serve 6 hungry adults. It takes about 1 full day (24 hours) to complete the finished pie—longer if you plan to freeze the pie. Plan ahead so your pie will be ready when you pack and leave for camp.

BILL ROMPA
Albany, Oregon

FAVORITE APPLE CRISP

5 cups sliced and peeled apples
¾ cup packed brown sugar
⅔ cup flour
⅔ cup oats
1 teaspoon ground cinnamon
¾ teaspoon ground nutmeg
⅓ cup butter

Butter an 8- or 9-inch square glass pan. Put apples in pan. Mix dry ingredients thoroughly. Cut in butter. Sprinkle topping over apples. Bake in preheated 350°F oven for about 40 minutes or until topping is golden brown and apples are tender.

LAURA NELSON
Providence, Utah

FRESH PEACH COBBLER

4 cups peaches, peeled and sliced
    (or you can use 1 large can
    of peaches)
2 cups sugar, divided
1 stick margarine
1 cup flour
2 teaspoons baking powder
½ teaspoon salt
¾ cup milk

Preheat oven to 325°F. Combine peaches and 1 cup sugar; set aside. (If using canned peaches, omit the sugar.) Melt margarine in a 9-by-13-inch glass dish. Combine all remaining ingredients; mix until all lumps are gone. Pour over margarine and spoon fruit on top of batter. Bake at 325°F for 50–60 minutes. Serves 8.

Note: Other fresh fruits may be used. Serve warm with cream, milk, ice cream, or frozen yogurt for a summer taste treat.

RON AND KAY DUNLAP
Onalaska, Washington

CHERRY DESSERT

½ pound graham crackers, crushed

1 cup butter or margarine, melted

½ cup sugar

2 3-ounce packages cream cheese, at room temperature

2 cups powdered sugar

1 large carton whipped dessert topping

1 can cherry (or blueberry) pie filling

Mix the graham cracker crumbs with melted butter and sugar. Line a 9-by-13-inch pan with this crust, saving ½ cup for topping. Chill.

Mix together the cream cheese and powdered sugar until soft and smooth. Fold in dessert topping. Pour mixture into crust. Pour a can of cherry pie filling over the top. Sprinkle the reserved crust mixture on top. Chill until ready to serve.

Variation: Make two 8-inch pies with this recipe. Use cherry pie filling in one crust, blueberry in the other.

STEVEN BOWEN
Moiese, Montana

WHITE CHOCOLATE TIRAMISU

2½ cups plus 2 tablespoons hot water

¼ cup instant espresso powder

6 tablespoons dark rum

8 ounces good-quality white chocolate, chopped

8 large egg yolks

1¾ cups powdered sugar

1¼ pounds cream cheese (2½ 8-ounce packages), at room temperature

4 large egg whites

¾ cup sugar

1½ cups chilled whipping cream

90 soft ladyfingers (4 3-ounce packages)

2 tablespoons unsweetened cocoa powder

Pour 2½ cups hot water into medium bowl. Add espresso powder and stir to dissolve. Stir in rum. Cool espresso mixture. Place chocolate in another medium bowl. Set bowl over saucepan of simmering water and stir until chocolate is melted and smooth.

Combine egg yolks, powdered sugar, and remaining 2 tablespoons water in another medium bowl. Set bowl over saucepan of simmering water and whisk constantly until mixture thickens slightly and reaches 160°F, about 6 minutes. Remove bowl from water. Using an electric mixer, beat egg yolk mixture until cool and thick. Using an electric mixer, beat cream cheese in large bowl until smooth, and then beat barely lukewarm chocolate into cream cheese. Fold the egg yolk mixture into the cream cheese mixture.

Using an electric mixer fitted with clean dry beaters, beat egg whites in another large bowl to soft peaks. Gradually add ¾ cup sugar, beating until stiff peaks form. Fold ⅓ of the beaten egg white mixture into the cream cheese mixture to lighten. Fold in the remaining egg white mixture. Beat whipping cream in medium bowl to

medium stiff peaks. Gently fold whipped cream into the cream cheese mixture, creating a mousse. Lightly dip ⅓ of the ladyfingers, one at a time, in espresso rum mixture and place in a single layer in the bottom of 13-by-9-by-2-inch glass baking dish. Spoon ⅓ of the mousse over ladyfingers, spreading evenly. Dip next ⅓ of the ladyfingers in espresso mixture and place atop mousse. Top lady fingers with another ⅓ of the mousse. Repeat with remaining ladyfingers, espresso mixture, and mousse. Sift cocoa powder over top of tiramisu. Cover and chill overnight.

EDITH FERRARIO
Central Point, Oregon

PEANUT BRITTLE

 1 cup sugar
 1 cup dark corn syrup
 1 tablespoon margarine
 Dash of salt
 2 cups raw peanuts
 1 teaspoon baking soda

Bring sugar, corn syrup, margarine, and salt to a boil, stirring constantly. Add the peanuts and bring the mixture to a boil over medium heat, stirring constantly. This will take about 16 minutes.

Remove pan from heat and add baking soda. The foam will double. Mix well. Spread the mixture quickly on a buttered cookie sheet. Cook and break into pieces. This will be very hot, so be careful.

PANSY BOWEN
Missoula, Montana

CHANTAL'S MAPLE SYRUP TREAT

A little bit of water (1 or 2 teaspoons)
2 Macintosh apples or Bosc pears, sliced into wedges
3 tablespoons of pure Vermont or Quebec maple syrup

Heat a cast-iron skillet over medium heat. Add water, then the fruit. Stir occasionally. When fruit starts to cook, add the maple syrup. Stir occasionally, and let caramelize slightly. Pour into bowls and serve. Also good over ice cream. You can dust lightly with cinnamon, but it really doesn't need anything more than good apples and syrup. Serves 2.

JACK AND CHANTAL
BUCHMILLER
Stamford, Connecticut

VELVEETA CHEESE FUDGE

1 pound Velveeta, cubed
1 pound margarine, cubed
4 pounds powdered sugar
1 cup powdered cocoa
1 tablespoon vanilla
2 cups nuts

Melt Velveeta and margarine over low heat or in microwave. Stir together powdered sugar and cocoa. Add gradually to Velveeta mixture and stir until smooth. Add vanilla and nuts. Spread in two 9-by-12-inch pans. Cover and refrigerate. Cut as needed.

Half of this makes a big pan!

PANSY BOWEN
Missoula, Montana

Dutch Oven Cooking

BY PHYLLIS SPEER

The Dutch oven is as much a part of American history as Thanksgiving turkey and apple pie. It was used by early colonists, by Lewis and Clark and their Corps of Discovery, and by settlers along the frontier trail. The Dutch oven is still the standard cooking vessel for the "cookie" and his chuck wagon on a modern-day cattle drive and for hunters and guides in many an elk camp.

The flexibility of the Dutch oven is phenomenal. It can be used on river rafting trips or wilderness elk hunts, in your backyard, or even at a Beverly Hills pot luck. Anywhere and anytime you want to cook out, the possibilities are endless. A Dutch oven is the most versatile cooking implement you can take along on a camping trip. Anything you can cook in your kitchen, you can cook in a Dutch oven. With the lid on, it can be used for baking, braising, roasting or stewing. This is accomplished by placing coals not only underneath the oven but also on its top. Hanging over a campfire, a Dutch oven may be used for pan frying or deep-frying or as a soup kettle. The flat lid can be used as a griddle for bacon, sausage, or pancakes. Once you begin to use a Dutch oven, it becomes an integral part of your cooking repertoire.

Many different kinds of pots are called Dutch ovens. However, the true Dutch oven has three legs and a lid with a raised lip around the edge to hold coals on the top. It is also called a camp oven or camp Dutch oven. A similar-shaped pot with a rounded lid and no legs is more properly called a kitchen oven.

The original Dutch ovens were made of cast iron. The only manufacturer producing cast-iron Dutch ovens in the United States today is Lodge Manufacturing. The family-owned business has been in existence since 1896 and continues to produce quality cast-iron Dutch ovens in many sizes. Modern technology has produced a Dutch oven from aluminum. While cast-iron and aluminum ovens look very similar, they cook differently; cast iron tends to heat up more slowly and retain the heat longer and has fewer hot spots, while aluminum heats up faster, cools down faster and doesn't seem to retain heat as long.

Dutch ovens also are categorized by their size. A #12 Dutch oven is 12 inches wide and holds about 6 quarts. A #10 Dutch oven is 10 inches wide and holds 4 quarts. Sizes range from #5 (1 pint) to #16 (12 quarts).

The old-fashioned way to cook in a Dutch oven is to use hardwood coals. These may be from the hearth or a campfire. When you use hardwood coals, allow at least forty-five minutes to an hour for your fire to make good cooking coals. It really wows them in camp when you pile the coals on to "cook the cobbler."

While not as romantic, a cleaner, easier way to cook in a Dutch oven is to use charcoal briquettes. With charcoal you don't need much fire or flame, so you can use your Dutch oven not only in camp but also in your backyard, at picnics, and even for tailgate parties. Charcoal briquettes burn much hotter and more slowly than hardwood coals.

When using briquettes, you usually need to place almost twice as many briquettes on the top of the oven as underneath it. For a #12 Dutch oven to cook at 325°F, you would place fifteen briquettes on top of the pot and nine underneath. To figure out how many briquettes to place on the lid, you add three to the number (#) on the oven indicating its size. Subtract three from the oven's number to determine how many briquettes go underneath. This formula may be used for any size Dutch oven to cook food at 325°F. For each 25°F you wish to increase the temperature, add three briquettes to the top and one underneath. This formula is a good one to follow and adjust as you get more familiar with your oven.

Not many extras are required for Dutch oven cooking, but a few items are recommended. First is a lid lifter to allow you to check how your meal is coming as it is cooking. They come in many lengths, shapes, and sizes. A pair of heat-resistant gloves is essential. Fireplace gloves, welding gloves, or gloves especially made for Dutch oven cooking are available. A small whisk broom will help to keep ashes out of the food you are cooking. A trivet provides a very handy place to set your lid while checking your food. For safety's sake, always have a bucket of water in close proximity to your Dutch oven cooking fire. Cold water can come in handy in case of an accident.

When using charcoal briquettes for Dutch oven cooking, you will need a charcoal chimney starter, long-handled tongs, and a protective cooking surface. (An oil pan, hog pan, metal drum lid, or metal cooking table may be used.) This helps to contain your heat source and ashes. As with any hobby, there are a number of other accessories you may acquire as you become more involved in Dutch oven cooking. However, the list above will get you started.

If you are a novice, begin with simple dishes to get the feel of using a Dutch oven. It won't take long until you will be trying your hand at more complex dishes. There are many good Dutch oven cookbooks available today. They contain step-by-step information to help you become an excellent Dutch oven chef. And, don't be afraid to try new dishes. Remember, anything you can cook in your kitchen, you can cook in your Dutch oven.

Cooking is not a science; it is an art. Each artist improves at his or her own pace. Try wowing your friends and family, whether at camp or in the backyard, with a delicious Dutch oven meal. The next time you have a get-together, don't make it just a pot luck, make it a lid liftin'! Once your guests have tasted your Dutch oven masterpiece, you will never again have to ring the dinner bell twice.

RMEF Life Member Phyllis Speer is regional education coordinator for the Arkansas Game & Fish Commission and a member of the Arkansas Dutch Oven Society. Besides cooking, she loves to hunt with bow and flintlock.

DUTCH OVEN AND CAMP COOKING

OZARK MOUNTAIN MAN BREAKFAST

1 pound bacon

1 onion, chopped

1 green pepper, chopped

1 30-ounce package frozen hash browns

Salt and pepper to taste

6 eggs, beaten

1½ cups grated cheddar cheese

Salsa or ketchup

Slice bacon in small pieces and brown in a #12 Dutch oven. Remove bacon pieces from oven and set aside. Cook onion and green pepper in bacon fat until soft. Add hash browns and salt and pepper to taste and cook until lightly browned. Sprinkle bacon on potatoes. Pour beaten eggs over bacon. Put top on Dutch oven and bake at 350°F until eggs are done. Sprinkle cheese over eggs and cover until cheese melts. Serve with salsa or ketchup.

PHYLLIS SPEER
Mountain Home, Arkansas

Camp Coffee

An old cowboy from Montana showed me how to make great coffee. First, use a clean coffeepot. Second, use good water. Most coffee is OK but some is just better. When water starts to simmer, put in the coffee. You will catch on as to the right amount. *Never let the coffee boil.* Let it come to a simmer (roll) and stir with a wooden spoon. You'll know when it's ready, and put in one cup of water to settle the grounds. That's all, now let 'em have at it.

JACK LUTCH
Wickenburg, Arizona

STUFFED MUSHROOMS A LA DARRELL

3 8-ounce packages large mushrooms

¼ cup Worcestershire sauce

½ stick pepperoni, finely chopped

8 ounces mozzarella cheese, shredded

1 cup seasoned bread crumbs

1 egg, beaten

½ cup finely chopped onion

Remove stems from mushroom caps. Set mushrooms aside. Mix remaining ingredients together with your hands so the mixture sticks together. If mixture seems not sticky enough, add another egg.

Fill each mushroom cap with a mound of mixture. Arrange mushroom caps in Dutch oven that has been coated with cooking spray. Cover and cook until cheese is bubbly.

PHYLLIS SPEER
Mountain Home, Arkansas

Hot Meat on Halt

This dish is easy to prepare in the wilderness over an open fire.

Take any cut of soft meat, rub surfaces with a bacon slice, salt, and pepper. Chop bacon, place on the meat, and wrap the meat in layer of clean gauze. Prepare a clay plaster, completely enclose the gauze with it, and place it inside thick ashes of burning fire. Maintain constant heat with surrounding fire ring. After 1 hour, turn the clay "pie" over and allow fire and ashes to die down. Cook for another hour. Remove and break clay from meat. Strain juices, pour over meat, and serve.

VADIM RIBAKOV
Smolensk, Russia

ELK ROAST

Large chunk of elk rump or a whole deer haunch, 6 to 12 pounds

1 garlic bulb

Rosemary

½ stick of butter

Parsnips

Potatoes

Onions

Carrots

Stab the roast with a pointed knife, and insert ¹⁄₁₆-inch slices of garlic into the openings ½–1 inch deep. The garlic slices should be placed about every 1–2 inches all over the roast. Heat a nonstick pan to high and melt some butter in the pan while you are rubbing copious amounts of rosemary into the roast. Heat the Dutch oven to 325°F. In the nonstick pan, brown the roast to a point it is almost burned. Once the roast is browned, place it and the remaining butter in a large Dutch oven or other tight roaster. Cook the roast for 2 hours (if it is a big, tough bull, reduce the heat and extend the time you plan to cook the meat). About an hour before dinner, add the vegetables. Parsnips take longer to cook, so they should be first into the roaster. If you want gravy, take the meat and vegetables out of the pan and make an outstanding gravy from the drippings in the roasting container. Any leftover roast will make great sandwiches.

JIM FICKE
Steamboat Springs, Colorado

ELK GRILLADE

½ cup water

Elk roast

Cajun seasoning

2–3 fresh tomatoes, sliced

1 green bell pepper, cored and sliced

1 large onion, sliced

Small, whole potatoes (optional)

Put water in a Dutch oven or electric skillet. Add elk roast. Make sure meat is not covered with water. Sprinkle liberally with Cajun seasoning. Layer tomatoes, bell pepper, and onion on top of the meat, completely covering it. If desired, put potatoes around the edges. Cook on very low heat at least 5 hours. If necessary, add more water.

RUTH WILSON
Jasper, Arizona

Canned Tomatoes

I use lots of canned tomatoes cooking at home and in camp. Although this doesn't qualify as a recipe, I recommend you try them in a couple of ways you may not have done. Chill canned whole tomatoes in your ice chest (or in a creek). Eaten right out of the can they are great with a sandwich, cheese, sausages, or any snack.

They make a nice dessert or sweet treat with the simple addition of a couple of tablespoons of sugar—again, right from the chilled can!

CHARLIE PIRTLE
Las Cruces, New Mexico

CABBAGE ELK

4 pounds elk steaks or roast (can also use deer, bear, or goose)
Yoshida's Original Gourmet Sauce
2–4 onions (depending on your taste for onions)
½ pound baby carrots
1 pound new potatoes (white or red)
1 medium head cabbage

Cut meat in 1-inch cubes or strips. Marinate in a resealable plastic bag with enough Yoshida's sauce to cover all surfaces of meat for a minimum of 2 hours, but overnight is OK too.

Grease a large Dutch oven with vegetable oil. Place meat from bag in the pot—do not use excess marinade. Place onions, baby carrots, and potatoes on top of the meat. Cut cabbage in wedges and place on top. Dribble ½ cup fresh Yoshida's sauce over cabbage. Cover and cook at 325°F for approximately 3 hours or until the kitchen smells very good.

PAUL SADLER
Bellingham, Washington

YANKEE ELK ROAST

2–3 pound elk roast

Salt and pepper to taste

8–10 potatoes, quartered

Assorted vegetables (carrots, bell peppers, onions, celery),
    cut into bite-size chunks

1 cup beef bouillon (low sodium is best)

Extra mushrooms

Grease the inside of a cast-iron Dutch oven. Put in roast, salted and peppered. Place potatoes and vegetables on top, then pour bouillon over it. Cover and bake at 325°F for approximately 2–3 hours. Remove roast and vegetables and put mushrooms in the remaining juice. Boil until juice thickens, then pour it over the roast and vegetables.

ELIZABETH HILL
Show Low, Arizona

SWISS ELK

5–6 elk steaks

Salt and pepper (be careful with the salt because the soup is quite salty)

1 tablespoon cooking oil

1–2 cans cream of mushroom soup

Extra canned mushrooms

Salt and pepper steaks and fry them in oil in Dutch oven. Pour in cans of soup, adding a little water to get gravy the right consistency. Cover and simmer until steaks are cooked through. Just before serving, add mushrooms. Serve with mashed potatoes.

ELIZABETH HILL
Show Low, Arizona

ELK HENLEY IN PUFFED PASTRY

1 stick butter (½ cup)

2 pounds elk meat, cut into 1-inch cubes

4 slices bacon, diced

2 large onions, chunked

1 pound fresh mushrooms, sliced

3 tablespoons flour

1 cup port wine

6 juniper berries

1 can beef broth

1 teaspoon thyme

Salt and pepper to taste

1 sheet puffed pastry

1 egg

1 tablespoon water

Melt butter in deep skillet. Add elk meat a few pieces at a time and brown. Remove from pan and set aside. Fry bacon until crisp. Set aside with meat. Add onions and mushrooms to pan and cook until golden brown. Stir in flour. Add port, juniper berries, broth, and thyme. Bring to a boil. Add elk and bacon and simmer for about 30 minutes. With a slotted spoon, place elk meat in a greased #12 deep Dutch oven. On medium heat cook sauce until it thickens. Salt and pepper to taste. Pour sauce over meat. Roll out pastry to fit Dutch oven. Put pastry on meat mixture. Glaze with an egg glaze, made by beating the egg with 1 tablespoon of water. Place lid on oven and bake at 400°F until crust is golden brown. Allow to cool for 5 to 10 minutes before serving.

Variation: To make this in the oven, use a greased, deep-sided casserole dish. Bake it at 400°F.

PHYLLIS SPEER
Mountain Home, Arkansas

MARV'S VENISON STROGANOFF A LA BUTTE, MONTANA

1 egg, beaten

1 cup cream or milk

2 pounds venison fillets

Flour for dredging

Cooking oil

1 can peas, drained, or 2 cups frozen peas

1 can tomatoes

1 large can cream of mushroom soup

Salt, seasoned salt, and pepper to taste

1 large package egg noodles

Thoroughly blend the egg and cream. Dip venison fillets into it and coat them with flour as you do in making country-fried steaks. Heat a covered Dutch oven to 360°F. Add enough cooking oil to brown the fillets. When thoroughly browned, transfer them to a large enough serving bowl to hold everything plus the sauce.

In the Dutch oven over moderate heat, combine the peas, tomatoes, mushroom soup, and seasonings. Turn down the heat and simmer the sauce until hot. Return the venison to the pan and cook long enough to let the flavors blend—at least 30 minutes.

While the steaks are cooking, cook the noodles according to package directions. Place them in a separate bowl, and serve noodles first, topped by the stroganoff.

A. J. CHRISTIANSEN
Kimball, Nebraska

ELK SCALLOPINI

2–3 pounds elk or venison

Flour for dredging

1 large onion, chopped

6 large garlic cloves, minced

2 tablespoons olive oil

2 28-ounce cans whole tomatoes

Bay leaves

Dried sweet basil

Dried oregano

2 stalks celery, chopped

2 large cans mushrooms

2 large bell peppers, chopped coarsely

1 large can sliced black olives

Salt and pepper

Cut meat into ½-inch-thick slices. Lightly flour, then brown. After cooling, slice meat into thin strips.

Sauté onion and garlic in 2 tablespoons olive oil. Place into large Dutch oven and add tomatoes, bay leaves, basil, and oregano, and simmer. Add celery, mushrooms, bell peppers, and black olives. Simmer for about 30 minutes. Add meat to the Dutch oven and place uncovered into the oven for about 2 hours at a low simmer (325°F–340°F). Season to taste. Serve over wide egg noodles with soft bread sticks brushed with garlic butter.

IRENE ADKINS
Sacramento, California

TERRI'S BBQ ELK

**3–4 pounds of a less tender cut of elk cut into small bite-size pieces
(or deer, antelope, moose, or sheep)**
1 tablespoon cooking oil
1 can beef broth
1 small can tomato paste
1 cup ketchup
1 garlic clove, minced
¾ cup packed brown sugar
½ cup chopped onion
½ cup vinegar
2 tablespoons prepared mustard
1½ teaspoons salt

In a Dutch oven, brown meat in oil. Add beef broth and bring to a boil. Reduce heat, cover, and simmer for 2 hours. Combine the tomato paste, ketchup, garlic, brown sugar, onion, vinegar, mustard, and salt; mix well. Pour over meat and bring to a boil. Reduce heat, cover, and simmer for 1 hour or until meat is tender. Serves 4 to 6.

TERRI JONES
Laramie, Wyoming

LAURA'S DUTCH OVEN CHILE VERDE

1 large marble-size piece beef fat
2 pounds lean stew meat (elk
    works great)
2 garlic cloves, smashed
2 beef bouillon cubes
2 cups water
2 14½-ounce cans stewed
    tomatoes
1 4-ounce can diced green chiles
1 teaspoon salt
1 teaspoon Cajun seasoning
Cooked white rice

Heat covered 10-inch Dutch oven over medium heat. Put in beef fat and heat, covered, until browned. Remove and discard remaining solid fat. This helps to flavor and season the inside of Dutch oven. Brown stew meat in Dutch oven. Add smashed garlic cloves and cook with meat a few minutes, stirring occasionally. Dissolve bouillon cubes in water and add to Dutch oven. Add all remaining ingredients and stir well. Bring to a simmer, cover, and cook at about 300°F for 2½–3 hours or until meat is tender. Serve over cooked white rice.

LAURA NELSON
Providence, Utah

Campfire Vegetables

For something different on your next camp trip, try fried squash. Start with chopped bacon and onions in a cast-iron flat-bottomed Dutch oven or frying pan until crispy brown. When about done, add sliced crookneck and zucchini squash and stir fry. Brown for a few minutes. Before serving, pour a little honey on the squash. Be sure to fix enough as hunters will come back for more.

JACK LUTCH
Wickenburg, Arizona

ELK CARBONADE

4–6 tablespoons vegetable oil or bacon fat

3 pounds elk stew meat, cubed

6 cups thickly sliced onions

1 tablespoon minced garlic

1 cup beef or chicken stock

1 12-ounce bottle of dark beer or stout

1 teaspoon ground black pepper

¼ cup molasses

2 tablespoons dried parsley

1 tablespoon dried thyme

2 bay leaves

2½ teaspoons cornstarch

3 tablespoons red wine vinegar

Salt and pepper to taste

Preheat oven to 300°F. Heat oil or bacon fat in a frying pan and brown elk in batches; do not crowd in pan. Remove meat to a Dutch oven. Add more oil as needed. When meat is browned, add oil, scrape pan, and cook onions at a moderate heat. Cook for 15 minutes stirring often, until golden brown. Add garlic, cook for 2–3 minutes more, and add to the meat in Dutch oven.

Pour stock into pan and scrape up bits stuck to bottom of pan. Pour into the Dutch oven. Add beer, pepper, molasses, parsley, thyme, and bay leaves to the Dutch oven. Stir and bring to a boil. Place the Dutch oven in the preheated oven and cook until meat is tender, 2–3 hours.

Remove Dutch oven from oven, place over a flame, and return to a simmer. Mix cornstarch and vinegar and stir into elk to thicken. Season to taste with salt and pepper. Can be served immediately, but tastes best the second day. Serves 6 to 8.

KEN LISTON
Helena, Montana

CYPRESS HILLS STEW

2 pounds stew meat (elk, deer, moose, beef, or whatever)
¼ cup dried onions
2 cans cream of something soup (mushroom, chicken, or celery)
1 can sliced mushrooms with liquid
½ cup sherry

Put meat in bottom of Dutch oven. Shake onions on top of meat. Spoon soup over meat evenly. Pour mushrooms on top of soup. Pour sherry over everything. Bake for 3–4 hours on low/medium heat (300°F). Stir occasionally in later stage of cooking.

This dish makes its own gravy as it cooks. You can add potatoes and veggies in the last half of cooking time if you like. We like it on egg noodles. It also works well in a roasting pan.

ROB YOUNG
Medicine Hat, Alberta

How to Cook a Turkey or Goose in Camp

Dig a hole about 2 feet deep and 1½ feet wide. Line the sides and bottom with rocks. Build a fire in the pit. When the fire is reduced to coals, dig out the coals and put the bird in, wrapped in a wet towel, sheet, shirt, etc.

Using leather gloves, move the rocks against the bird and backfill behind the rocks, working upward. Top with rocks, then shovel coals on top and go hunting. In 6 to 8 hours your bird will fall off the bone and be very moist.

P.S.: Kiss the shirt good-bye.

ROMAN DODSON
North Hills, California

LAURA'S DUTCH OVEN STEW

1 large marble-size piece beef fat

2 pounds lean stew meat (elk works great)

1 large onion, chopped

1 large garlic clove, smashed

2 beef bouillon cubes

2½ cups water

1 10¾-ounce can cream of mushroom soup

1 tablespoon seasoned salt

3 large carrots, peeled and cut into 2-inch lengths

4 medium potatoes, peeled and quartered

Heat a covered 10-inch (12-inch works well, too) Dutch oven over medium heat. Put in beef fat and heat, covered, until browned. Remove and discard remaining solid fat. This helps to season and flavor the inside of Dutch oven. Brown stew meat in Dutch oven, stirring occasionally. Add onions and garlic. Cook and stir with meat until onions are tender. Stir in beef bouillon cubes dissolved in water, then add mushroom soup and seasoning. Stir and bring to a simmer. Cook in covered Dutch oven at about 300°F for about 2½ hours or until meat is tender. Add vegetables in last 45 minutes.

LAURA NELSON
Providence, Utah

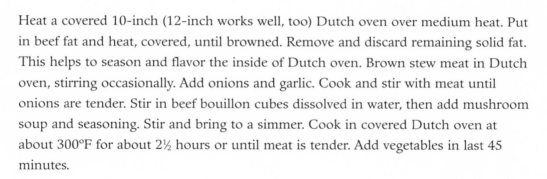

LAURA'S DUTCH OVEN STROGANOFF

1 large marble-size piece beef fat

2 pounds lean stew meat (elk works great)

1 large onion, chopped

2 beef bouillon cubes

2 cups water

1 10¾-ounce can cream of mushroom soup

1 teaspoon salt

¼ teaspoon pepper

1 teaspoon paprika

1 can sliced mushrooms (optional)

Cooked white rice

Heat a covered 10-inch Dutch oven over medium heat. Put in beef fat and heat, covered, until browned. Remove and discard the solid fat. This helps to season and flavor the inside of Dutch oven. Brown meat in Dutch oven, stirring occasionally. Stir in onions and cook with meat, stirring occasionally until onions are tender. Add beef bouillon dissolved in water, then add mushroom soup and seasonings. Add mushrooms, if desired. Stir and bring to a simmer. Cover and cook at about 300°F for about 2½ hours, or until meat is tender. Served over cooked white rice.

LAURA NELSON
Providence, Utah

SHEPHERD'S PIE

**5 medium potatoes (wash and pare off the rough spots, leaving
  the skin on)**
2 pounds ground elk
1 tablespoon cooking oil
1 medium onion, peeled and diced
1 clove garlic, minced
1 teaspoon chili powder
¼ teaspoon cumin
4 beef bouillon cubes, or 4 teaspoons beef bouillon granules
1 heaping tablespoon flour
Salt and pepper to taste
Dash of paprika

Quarter the potatoes, cover with water, and cook them in a heavy saucepan at a low
boil for approximately 20 minutes.

Brown elk in oil in a Dutch oven. When it's nearly done, add the onion, garlic,
and spices. Continue to cook until the onion is cooked through. Add enough potato
water (they should be ready to drain by now) to cover the meat mixture, and add the
bouillon. Bring to a high simmer.

Make a paste with flour and water, adding slowly to the bubbling meat mixture. It
will thicken as it cooks.

Mash the potatoes, and spoon directly onto the bubbling meat and gravy, nearly
covering it. Add salt and pepper, a dash of paprika, and bake uncovered in a medium
oven until the gravy begins to bubble through, approximately 40 minutes. Serve with
a vegetable or a salad, crusty bread, and you have a hearty meal for two hungry
hunters!

JOHN R. HARVIEUX
Osceola, Wisconsin

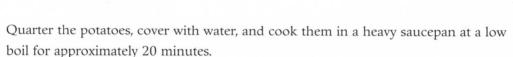

MULE SKINNER PIE

2 pounds ground meat

2 onions, chopped

4 cloves garlic, minced

2 tablespoons Worcestershire sauce

1 package taco seasoning

1 10-ounce package frozen corn

1 large green pepper, chopped

1 4-ounce jar pimientos

1 can diced tomatoes and chiles (Rotel recommended)

1 8-ounce can tomato sauce

1 can red beans, drained

1 teaspoon salt

1 teaspoon pepper

Sauté meat, onion, garlic, and Worcestershire until lightly brown in a #12 Dutch oven that has been coated with vegetable spray. Add taco seasoning and remaining ingredients, stirring with each addition. Heat thoroughly until bubbling.

TOPPING

2 cups corn bread mix

1½ cups milk

1 egg

2 teaspoons honey

1 cup sliced ripe olives

1½ cups grated cheddar cheese

1 teaspoon chopped jalapeño
   peppers

Mix corn bread mix with milk, egg, and honey. Then add olives, cheese, and peppers. Pour topping over mixture in Dutch oven. Bake at 400°F for about 30–45 minutes or until corn bread is golden brown.

PHYLLIS SPEER
Mountain Home, Arkansas

JETTIE MAE'S PANHANDLER SPAGHETTI

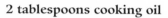

2 tablespoons cooking oil

1½ pounds ground chuck

1 onion, chopped

1 green pepper, chopped

1 can whole kernel corn

1 28-ounce can diced tomatoes

1 can sliced mushrooms

4 beef bouillon cubes

1 teaspoon Italian seasoning

1 8-ounce package grated cheddar cheese

Salt and pepper to taste

1 10-ounce package spaghetti

Spray Dutch oven with vegetable spray. Add oil. Brown meat. Add onions and green peppers. Cook until vegetables are soft. Add remaining ingredients, reserving half of the cheese. Do not cook spaghetti—break and put in the Dutch oven dry. (It works, I promise.) Put lid on oven. Place coals underneath oven and on top. Cook at 350°F for 30 minutes. Check for doneness. Add remaining cheese to top. Replace lid to melt cheese. Serve.

PHYLLIS SPEER
Mountain Home, Arkansas

DEER MEAT PIES

2 teaspoons shortening
2 teaspoons all-purpose flour
1 pound ground pork
1 pound ground venison
1 large onion, finely chopped
6 green onions, chopped
1 tablespoon chopped fresh parsley
1 teaspoon salt
¼ teaspoon rubbed sage
⅛ teaspoon pepper
Dash of red pepper
Pastry (recipe follows)
Cooking oil

Combine shortening and flour in a large Dutch oven. Cook over medium heat, stirring constantly, until roux is the color of a copper penny. Add pork, venison, onions, parsley, and seasonings. Cook over medium heat until meat is browned and onions are tender, stirring occasionally. Drain well and cool.

Make pastry and divide into 22 equal portions. Roll out each portion into a 5-inch circle. Place about 2 tablespoons meat mixture in center of each circle, and fold pastry in half. Moisten edges with water and press with a fork to seal.

Heat 1 inch of oil to 375°F. Fry pies in hot oil until golden, turning once. Drain on paper towels.

PASTRY

4 cups all-purpose flour

2 teaspoons baking powder

1 teaspoon salt

½ cup shortening, melted

½ cup plus 2 tablespoons milk

2 eggs, slightly beaten

Combine flour, baking powder, and salt. Add melted shortening, stirring until blended. Combine milk and eggs, stirring well. Pour milk mixture into flour mixture; stir just until blended, adding more milk if necessary. Makes enough pastry for 22 meat pies.

KATHY MURPHY
Oviedo, Florida

Dutch Oven Cola Roast

Coca-Cola is the key to this recipe.

To a 12-inch Dutch oven add two Coca-Colas, a half bottle of barbecue sauce, some water, and a big roast—beef, elk, or deer. Bring liquid to a boil, add potato chunks, carrots, mushroom, celery, onions, and garlic, and let it boil gently for 3 or 4 hours, adding water to keep from boiling it dry. You can also add rice or barley to thicken the mix, and serve. The acid in the Coke breaks down the fibers in the meat and makes it very tender, and gives it a distinctive taste that is very well received by hungry hunters. It can be cooked in a large pan or even a pressure cooker, but a Dutch oven is very handy for a campsite cooker.

HARLAN WHITE
Canyonville, Oregon

DUTCH OVEN LASAGNA

1 pound ground venison

1 large onion, chopped

4 large cloves garlic, sliced

1 can mushroom stems and pieces

1 small can sliced ripe olives

1 teaspoon dried oregano

1 teaspoon salt

½ teaspoon pepper

1 32-ounce jar spaghetti sauce

1 egg, slightly beaten

1 15-ounce container ricotta cheese (or cottage cheese)

1 box lasagna noodles, uncooked

1 12-ounce package grated mozzarella cheese

½ cup grated Parmesan cheese

Spray a #12 Dutch oven with vegetable spray. Brown venison in the Dutch oven. Add onions and garlic and cook until onions are soft. Transfer from oven to large bowl. Add mushrooms, olives, oregano, salt, pepper, and spaghetti sauce to the bowl and mix well. In another small bowl mix eggs with ricotta cheese. Pour a thin layer of the meat sauce mixture in bottom of the Dutch oven. Add a layer of lasagna noodles (do not cook noodles!), a layer of ricotta cheese, and mozzarella cheese. Repeat layers twice, ending with meat sauce mixture. Sprinkle Parmesan cheese on top. Bake in the Dutch oven for about 45 minutes with nine coals on bottom and fifteen coals on top.

PHYLLIS SPEER
Mountain Home, Arkansas

VENISON MEAT LOAF DINNER

2 pounds ground venison

1 pound ground pork

1 large onion, finely chopped

4 cloves garlic, finely minced

1 cup seasoned bread crumbs

2 eggs, slightly beaten

½ cup beef broth

½ cup ketchup

1½ teaspoons salt

1 teaspoon pepper

2 tablespoons chopped fresh parsley

Vegetables to fill hole in center of oven (I use potatoes, carrots, and
    brussels sprouts)

Additional ketchup to cover meat loaf

Mix first eleven ingredients in large bowl. Mix well. Spray a #12 Dutch oven with
vegetable spray. Put meat mixture in the Dutch oven and spread out in a ring against
the sides of the oven, leaving a well in the center. Place vegetables in the center well.
Add salt and pepper to taste. Add additional ketchup to top of meatloaf, covering
well. Cook at 375°F for about 1½ hours.

PHYLLIS SPEER
Mountain Home, Arkansas

DUTCH OVEN SLOPPY JOES

1 pound ground beef

Salt and pepper

1 red onion, diced

3 cloves garlic, diced

1 green bell pepper, sliced

1 red bell pepper, sliced

1 can sliced olives

1 large can Manwich sauce

1 can large biscuits

Grated cheese

Fry the ground beef and season with salt and pepper. Add onion, garlic, and peppers and cook until tender. Add olives and sauce. Let simmer for about an hour. Sprinkle cheese on top. Place biscuits on top and bake until brown.

JIM WEBER
Helena, Montana

Charlie's Chili

Chili recipes are a dime a dozen—and I never ate a bowl of chili I didn't like! My recipe isn't exotic, but I think it's mighty good!

I use game meat almost exclusively and have used deer, elk, antelope, oryx, bear, and sheep, but the best batch I ever made was made with javelina!

In a deep pot or Dutch oven, fry bacon (strips or pieces) until brown. Remove from pot. Add about 2–4 pounds of ground meat (coarse ground seems to taste best). Stir meat until well browned and add a large chopped onion and 5–6 cloves minced garlic. Add salt to taste and crumbled browned bacon, and then add 3–4 heaping tablespoons pure ground red chile. (Here in New Mexico, we use lots of chile. The heat index of the chile will vary—as well as the tolerance of the consumer of the dish. I feel that the pure chile makes a better pot of chili than using a commercial chili powder.) I add cumin and oregano to my chili.

After the ground chile has blended with the meat and has given it its rich, red color, I add a large can of diced tomatoes and their juice. Simmer for 2–3 hours. I prefer my chili not to be too soupy, but if it is too dry to suit you, an additional small can of diced tomatoes may be added. I think that adds more richness than water would.

CHARLIE PIRTLE
Las Cruces, New Mexico

DUTCH OVEN LAYERED MEXICAN CASSEROLE

1 pound ground venison
Salt and pepper to taste
1 red onion, diced
2 4½-ounce cans green chiles, diced
1 box Spanish rice
6 large corn tortillas
1 cup salsa
1 10-ounce can green chile sauce
3 cups cheddar and/or Jack cheese
1 fresh tomato, diced
1 can olives, sliced
1 cup fresh grated lettuce
Sour cream to taste

Get your oven hot. Fry the ground meat and season with salt and pepper. Drain the fat. Add onion and diced green chiles. Mix well. Remove meat mixture. Cook Spanish rice according to directions on the box. Remove rice. Wipe your Dutch oven clean. Place two tortillas in bottom of oven. Spread half of meat mixture on top of tortillas. Pour salsa on top of meat. Place two more tortillas on top of meat mixture. Spread rice on the tortillas. Add last two tortillas. Place remaining meat mixture on top. Pour green chile sauce on top of meat. Sprinkle grated cheese on top and bake. Just before serving, sprinkle diced tomato and olives on top. Add a little more cheese and lettuce. Bake until cheese is just melted. Top individual servings with sour cream.

JIM WEBER
Helena, Montana

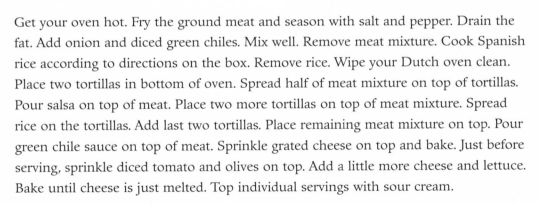

TACO SOUP

4 strips bacon

1½ pounds ground beef

1 large onion, chopped (use red onion for color)

1 28-ounce can tomatoes with juice, chopped

1 15-ounce can kidney beans

1 17-ounce can whole kernel corn with liquid

1 8-ounce can tomato sauce

1 package taco seasoning

1 can beef broth

1 15-ounce can pinto beans

1 jalapeño pepper, chopped

½ green bell pepper, chopped

3 cups water

1 cup sliced fresh mushrooms

TOPPINGS

½ cup shredded Pepper Jack cheese

1 cup Mark's Fresh Salsa (recipe follows)

½ cup sour cream

Tortilla chips, crumbled

Grease oven with bacon then discard, then brown ground beef and add the other ingredients. Simmer for 1 hour and serve with your choice of toppings.

MARK'S FRESH SALSA

5 fresh medium tomatoes, seeded and diced

1 medium red onion, chopped

1 jalapeño pepper, chopped (serrano chiles can
    be used for more bite)

⅓ cup olive oil

1 cup cilantro, minced

Juice of 1 lime

3 cloves garlic, minced

Combine all ingredients and mix well.

MARK MARSH
Coalville, Utah

Pork Chops over Scalloped Potatoes

Slice potatoes up like poker chips, peeled and about ⅛ inch thick. In a 12-inch Dutch oven, add a layer of these, then a layer of sliced onions. On top of that add a layer of flour and some shredded cheese. This layer should be about ¼ inch thick. Alternate this combination until an inch from the top, then lay on 12 pork chops, which have been browned on the lid, turned over on the fire. You need to add milk or mushroom soup to the layers of potato, onion, and cheese and flour until it is visible at the top of the layers. Cook this very slowly by burying it in a pit at the edge of your fire, on top of some coals, with others around the pot, and some on the lid, and about 3 inches of dirt over the entire oven. The fat from the cooking pork chops will flavor the entire batch of scalloped potatoes and will be a really nice meal to come home to after a hard day of hunting. Just don't add too much heat, or you will boil it dry and have a disaster.

HARLAN WHITE
Canyonville, Oregon

SQUIRREL STEW

2 tablespoons olive oil

3 cloves garlic, minced

2 squirrels, cleaned and cut into pieces

¼ cup flour

1 teaspoon salt

½ teaspoon pepper

2 large onions, chopped

4 cups water

4 beef bouillon cubes

2 large potatoes, cubed

2 large carrots, diced

2 stalks celery, diced

2 cups frozen lima beans

2 14½-ounce cans diced tomatoes

2 cups frozen corn kernels

1 teaspoon Worcestershire sauce

1½ teaspoons sugar

3 tablespoons flour

½ cup cold water

Heat olive oil and garlic in a large Dutch oven. Dredge squirrels in ¼ cup flour, salt, and pepper. Brown squirrels in oil. Add onions and cook until soft. Add 4 cups water, bouillon cubes, potatoes, carrots, and celery. Cover and simmer 1 hour. Add lima beans, tomatoes, corn, Worcestershire sauce, and sugar. Cover and simmer 30 minutes. Mix 3 tablespoons flour with ½ cup cold water. Stir until smooth. Add to stew and simmer until slightly thickened. Season to taste with salt and pepper.

MARY ANNE LECCE
Collinsville, Illinois

LAURA'S DUTCH OVEN CAJUN BBQ CHICKEN

About 8 chicken thighs, skin removed
1 18-ounce bottle barbecue sauce
Cajun seasoning to taste
Warm water

Heat a covered 10-inch Dutch oven (a 12-inch one will also work) over medium heat. Put 2 chicken skins, removed from thighs, in Dutch oven. Heat, covered, over medium heat until skins are browned. Remove and discard the skin. This helps to season and flavor the inside of Dutch oven. Put the chicken thighs in Dutch oven—crowd them in close. Season chicken thighs with Cajun seasoning to taste. Go easy at first with seasoning, if you are not sure how much to put on. You can always add more later. Pour the whole bottle of barbecue sauce over the chicken. Fill the bottle halfway with warm water. Put lid on tight and shake well. Pour around inside edge of Dutch oven. Cover and cook at about 300°F for about 2½ hours, or until chicken thighs are very tender. Serve thighs with cooked barbecue sauce poured over them.

LAURA NELSON
Providence, Utah

Quick Camp Bread

For a quick and easy camp bread, try a cinnamon and raisin bagel by Thomas'. They come sliced. Just warm a bagel in a cast-iron skillet with bacon grease. They are made like bread used to be made. They can also be used for sandwiches.

JACK LUTCH
Wickenburg, Arizona

BAKED CHICKEN AND RICE

1 cup uncooked rice
1 chicken, cut into serving pieces
1 package dry onion soup mix
1 can chicken broth
1 can cream of mushroom soup
Water

Place rice in a 10-inch Dutch oven. Place chicken on top of the rice. Sprinkle dry soup mix on top of chicken. Mix 1 can of water with broth and cream soups. Pour mixture over the chicken and bake with coals on top and bottom of Dutch oven for at least 1 hour.

JIM JUSTICE
Boise, Idaho

BARBECUED BEANS

1 pound bacon slices, cut in thirds
1 large onion, chopped
5 15½-ounce cans pork and beans
2¼ cups brown sugar
¼ cup Worcestershire sauce
1 12-ounce bottle ketchup
¼ cup prepared mustard
2 teaspoons liquid smoke

Fry bacon in Dutch oven until cooked crisp. Add onion and sauté until clear. Stir in beans, then add remaining ingredients. Bake at 325°F for 3 hours or until cooked down to desired consistency.

JIM JUSTICE
Boise, Idaho

CHICKEN WITH BEER AND NOODLES

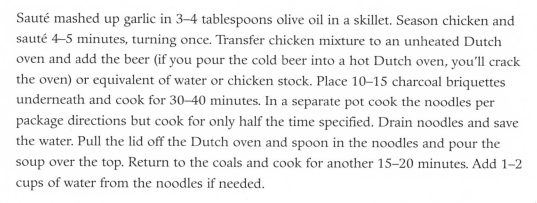

6–8 cloves garlic

Olive oil

1–2 boneless chicken breasts

Salt and pepper or other seasoning

2 cans beer

1 12-ounce package wide egg noodles

1 26-ounce can cream soup (either mushroom, celery, or chicken)

Sauté mashed up garlic in 3–4 tablespoons olive oil in a skillet. Season chicken and sauté 4–5 minutes, turning once. Transfer chicken mixture to an unheated Dutch oven and add the beer (if you pour the cold beer into a hot Dutch oven, you'll crack the oven) or equivalent of water or chicken stock. Place 10–15 charcoal briquettes underneath and cook for 30–40 minutes. In a separate pot cook the noodles per package directions but cook for only half the time specified. Drain noodles and save the water. Pull the lid off the Dutch oven and spoon in the noodles and pour the soup over the top. Return to the coals and cook for another 15–20 minutes. Add 1–2 cups of water from the noodles if needed.

JIM JUSTICE
Boise, Idaho

CALABACITAS CON POLLO Y CHILE

Chicken (boneless breasts are easiest)
Cooking oil
Green chile (fresh, frozen, or canned), diced
Onion, diced
Squash (almost any kind—zucchini, yellow, Mexican, etc.)
Salt, pepper, and garlic
Cheese (your favorite kind, grated)

Cut chicken into strips or chunks. Lightly brown in enough oil to prevent sticking. When chicken is ready, add diced green chile to taste. Add diced onion. Cut squash into disks and add to pot. Season with salt, pepper, and garlic. Simmer until chicken is tender. Shortly before serving, remove from heat and cover with lots of grated cheese. Replace lid until cheese melts completely.

Quantity of ingredients is not given, as it matters little. Use more or less as you choose. A nice variation is to add canned or frozen corn to the pot during the simmering process.

CHARLIE PIRTLE
Las Cruces, New Mexico

DUTCH OVEN CHICKEN ENCHILADAS

1½ pounds boneless chicken breasts, cubed

2 tablespoons oil

1 bunch green onions, sliced

1 4-ounce can diced green chiles

1 10-ounce can ripe olives, sliced

2 tablespoons cumin seeds

Salt and pepper to taste

2 cups sour cream

9 flour tortillas

1 pound shredded Monterey Jack cheese

½ pound shredded mild cheddar cheese

1 15-ounce can crushed tomatoes

In a skillet lightly brown chicken pieces in oil. Add green onions and cook until tender. Add green chiles, olives, cumin seeds, salt, and pepper. Mix well. Add sour cream to mixture. Set aside.

Spray a #12 Dutch oven with vegetable spray. Cover bottom with tortillas. Add a layer of chicken mixture. Top with a layer of cheese and then a layer of tomatoes. Repeat layers. Cover with tortillas and finish with a layer of cheese.

Bake in the Dutch oven at 350°F for about 40–45 minutes. Let stand 10 minutes before serving. Serve with favorite salsa.

PHYLLIS SPEER
Mountain Home, Arkansas

Sociable Pinto Beans

These recipes for pinto beans make "sociable" beans, meaning the snappers have been removed. To prepare for cooking, put dry beans in a Dutch oven in the morning. Remove dirt, mice thingies, etc., and cover with water. Soak for 2 hours. Discard water and rinse beans and Dutch oven, return beans to Dutch oven, cover with an inch of water and add salt. At least twice more during the day, drain, rinse, soak in water with salt. Next morning, do it again. At noon change the water one more time and add salt. Then you are ready to cook. Use lots of coals on lid of Dutch oven. Cooking time varies from 2 to 4 hours, depending on variables such as altitude and source of coals. Number of servings depends on how hungry your gang is.

Sometimes I use a stove-top "Dutch oven" on a Coleman stove, keeping the pot boiling. Cooking time is less.

Best-Ever Pinto Beans (vegetarian)

2–3 cups of dry beans soaked
    overnight, salted
Big handful of dried minced onion

Cook until done. Add 1 package of Knorr vegetable soup and recipe mix. Finish cooking, 10 minutes.

Variation: For perfect beans, with ham, follow the same procedure as above, but also add 1 tablespoon of black ground pepper and ham, or a smoked pork shank or hock before starting to cook. Do not add the soup mix.

A. GRANT MACOMBER
Applegate, California

SWEET POTATOES ON AN OPEN FIRE

3 large sweet potatoes or yams, cut into pieces (not too small)

½ stick butter

½ cup brown sugar

3 teaspoons ground cinnamon

On a piece of aluminum foil, place cut-up sweet potatoes. Put butter, brown sugar, and cinnamon on top. Close the aluminum foil like a package and place on hot coals or on a grill (this is better when done in the flames of a campfire). Turn package over after 5 minutes. Check often so they don't burn. If done on a grill, place on medium heat for 20 minutes. Unwrap and enjoy.

MARY KAMP
Kempton, Pennsylvania

Dutch Oven Cottontail

Put olive oil or bacon grease in a flat-bottom Dutch oven. Get the oil bubbling hot. Take 2 or 3 cottontails, cut up, and flour (seasoned with salt and pepper). Brown the rabbit pieces in the Dutch oven for about 30 minutes. After this put 1 or 2 cups of liquid in the oven. This can be water, beer, or wine. Put in at least one quartered onion and 1 or 2 chopped garlic cloves. Cover and leave the oven on the grill for about 2 hours. You can tell when it's done. Be sure and stir and check the liquid. Cook plenty, as your guests will want more.

JACK LUTCH
Wickenburg, Arizona

SPICY SOUTHWEST POTATOES

1 pound bacon, chopped

Potatoes, unpeeled and thickly sliced

1 red onion, chopped

½ green bell pepper, chopped

1 red bell pepper, chopped

1 jalapeño pepper, chopped fine

1 cup finely chopped cilantro

1½ pounds Pepper Jack cheese, shredded

Cover bottom of a Dutch oven with pieces of bacon, then layer potatoes, onion, bell peppers, jalapeño, and chopped cilantro. Cook until potatoes are done. Then add Pepper Jack cheese. Heat for 10 minutes and serve.

MARK MARSH
Coalville, Utah

Chile Roasted Elk

Here is a simple and tasty way to prepare elk roast (or any game roast). It provides the moisture needed in drier game meat. Insert garlic slivers into slits pierced deeply into roast. Season to your taste. Sear roast in a large pot with a small amount of oil. This can be done with or without flour. Pour a can of diced tomatoes with juice over the roast. Layer slices of onions on top of the tomatoes. Top this off with strips of green chile, frozen or canned. (If fresh chile is used, it should be roasted and peeled.)

The roast can be cooked in a Crock-Pot, on top of the stove, or in camp on wood coals in a Dutch oven.

CHARLIE PIRTLE
Las Cruces, New Mexico

LAURA'S DUTCH OVEN POTATOES

½ pound bacon, diced

2 large onions, chopped

Potatoes, peeled and sliced ¼-inch thick

Seasoned salt to taste

Pepper to taste

1 12-ounce can evaporated milk

1 can cream of mushroom soup

Broccoli crowns, stems removed (enough to cover potatoes)

3 cups grated cheddar cheese

Heat Dutch oven over medium heat. Brown bacon until almost done, stirring occasionally. Stir in onions and cook until tender, stirring occasionally. Scoop out bacon-onion mixture. Fill Dutch oven ⅓ full of sliced potatoes. Sprinkle heavily with seasoned salt and medium with pepper. Top with half of the bacon-onion mixture. Add more sliced potatoes until Dutch oven is ⅔ full. Sprinkle heavily with seasoned salt and medium with pepper. Top with remaining bacon-onion mixture. Pour canned milk evenly over the top. Spread mushroom soup on very top. Cook, covered, at 350°F for about 1 hour or until potatoes are tender. Cover top of potatoes with broccoli crowns. Cover and cool 10 more minutes. Put grated cheese on top of broccoli and cook, covered, until cheese melts—just a few minutes.

LAURA NELSON
Providence, Utah

DUTCH OVEN SWEET CARROTS

1 bag baby carrots
Water
1 cup brown sugar
2 tablespoons butter

Pour enough water in the Dutch oven to cover the carrots. Cook until tender. Drain the water. Add sugar and butter. Stir and serve.

JIM WEBER
Helena, Montana

Herter's Model Perfect Green Enchiladas

This recipe is from my memory, as it appeared in one of those great old Herter's catalogs. Seems like almost everything listed was called Herter's Model Perfect So-and-So. This is another good camp meal—quick, easy, and good! Again, I don't list quantities, as they are not critical.

Brown ground meat in a deep pot or Dutch oven. When meat is cooked, add salt, 5–6 cloves garlic, cumin, a large diced onion, and diced frozen or canned green chile. (If fresh chile is used it should be roasted and peeled.) While the meat mixture is cooking, dice more onion and grate cheese for topping. Drain most of the liquid from the meat and add a 16-ounce container of sour cream. Stir into meat until blended.

When ready to serve, heat corn tortillas in a skillet containing hot oil. Place a tortilla on a plate and layer on the meat mixture with chopped onion and grated cheese. Repeat layers and top with shredded lettuce and chopped tomato. Two or three layers of these will stick to your ribs and help you up the mountain the next day!

CHARLIE PIRTLE
Las Cruces, New Mexico

DUTCH OVEN HUNTIN' CAMP CORN BREAD

2 8½-ounce boxes Jiffy Corn Muffin Mix

½ pound butter

1 16-ounce can creamed corn

1 4½-ounce can diced green chiles

1 red bell pepper, diced

1 cup sour cream

3 eggs, beaten

1 cup cream cheese

Preheat Dutch oven. Mix all ingredients together except cream cheese. Pour mixed ingredients in the oven. Chop cream cheese into little pieces and drop into the mix. Let cook until a toothpick comes clean. This corn bread will be really moist and is fantastic served with buffalo wings or chili.

JIM WEBER
Helena, Montana

OLD-FASHIONED CORN BREAD

1 cup white flour
1 cup yellow cornmeal
3 teaspoons baking powder
1 teaspoon salt
¼ cup brown sugar
¼ cup shortening
1 egg
1 cup buttermilk (or more)

This is a proven corn bread recipe—you don't need to add all that junk to make it good. Of course, it's best when made in a cast-iron Dutch oven. Build a good fire to make coals. Heat the oven and lid, greasing it with bacon fat or shortening. Mix everything together and pour in the corn bread mixture to about 1 inch thick or less. Set oven on a *few* coals, put on the lid, and load the lid with coals. Turn the Dutch oven and lid every 5 minutes to distribute the heat evenly. It's easy to have too many coals on the bottom, so use caution. *Don't crack the lid until you smell corn bread.* If it's too hot on the bottom, take oven off coals. Serve with jelly or honey.

JACK LUTCH
Wickenburg, Arizona

BEER BREAD

3 cups self-rising flour
3 tablespoons sugar
1 beer

Mix and put in iron frying pan or Dutch oven to bake. If barbecuing, put some coals on top of Dutch oven.

ROMAN DODSON
North Hills, California

Stew in a Bag

Put a 6-quart pot on the stove or over a campfire. Spray the bottom of the pan with cooking spray and then take a pound of lean ground meat and break it up into small chunks. Brown it, and while it's browning take a large onion, 2 cloves garlic, and 3 stalks celery, chop them into small chunks and dump them in with the cooking meat.

Stir now and then. Once it starts to sizzle, throw in 3 quarts water. Wash at least one good-sized potato per person in the group and cut the potatoes up into 1-inch chunks, then dump them into the pot. Once it comes to a boil, taste the broth, and add salt and pepper to taste as needed. Next, dump in a can of stewed tomatoes and a small bag of small carrots. If you have corn on the cob, cut off the corn and dump it in, too. Let this come to a boil again. (Whatever you like for veggies can be put into this stew.)

Once the carrots are soft, everything will be done cooking, too. Then take 1 cup instant potatoes and stir it into the broth, a little at a time. You will end up with a very flavorful, thick stew. The whole carrots will be intact and so will the potatoes and celery. Serve with crackers or bread.

Helpful hint: If you should put in too much salt, drop in a leaf or two of lettuce and as it cooks down, the lettuce will absorb the salt.

This stew can be all cut up before you ever leave home and put in plastic bags. All you need to do then is put the meat in the pot, add the water, season to taste, open the bag and dump. Once the water boils, 1 more hour and dinner is ready.

SALLY KEMPLE
Portland, Oregon

CHARLIE'S BISCUITS

2 cups flour
2 tablespoons sugar
½ teaspoon baking soda
2 teaspoons baking powder
½ teaspoon salt
¼ cup oil or drippings
1 cup buttermilk or sour milk

Mix dry ingredients, then stir in oil and buttermilk. (Dry buttermilk mix works well in camp and/or you can sour fresh or canned milk with vinegar.) Mix quickly into a soft dough. Pat or roll to about ½ inch thick and cut with cutter.

Have some additional oil in your pan or Dutch oven. Turn each biscuit in the oil so that tops are greased. Crowd biscuits into your pan or Dutch oven. Baking time in your oven is about 15–18 minutes at 450°F. Dutch oven cooking time is about 10–12 minutes, but will vary depending on wood, wind, etc.

CHARLIE PIRTLE
Las Cruces, New Mexico

DUTCH OVEN COCONUT PIE

2 cups milk

1 cup sugar

4 eggs

½ cup flour

6 tablespoons butter or margarine

1 tablespoon vanilla extract

½ teaspoon salt

1 cup shredded coconut

2 tablespoons cinnamon

Use a mixer to blend all ingredients. Pour into a greased 10-inch Dutch oven and cook for 1 hour. Sprinkle with cinnamon when done. This pie makes its own crust as it cooks. Serve the pie warm.

JIM WEBER
Helena, Montana

DOC McCOY'S PEACH COBBLER

2 28-ounce cans sliced peaches in
heavy syrup

1 stick butter

1 package yellow cake mix,
butter recipe

Peach Schnapps, bourbon or brandy
(optional, but a nice addition)

Spray a #12 cast-iron Dutch oven with vegetable spray. Pour peaches in oven and sprinkle dry cake mix over peaches. *Do not stir!!!* Slice butter and place on top of dry cake mix. *Do not stir!!!* Sprinkle about ⅓ cup liquor on top if desired. Bake at 400°F for about 45 minutes, or until golden brown.

PHYLLIS SPEER
Mountain Home, Arkansas

PUMPKIN PRALINE PIE

1 16-ounce can pumpkin

1 14-ounce can condensed milk

2 eggs

1 teaspoon ground cinnamon

½ teaspoon ground nutmeg

½ teaspoon ginger

½ teaspoon salt

1 pie crust

½ cup pecans

3 tablespoons brown sugar

3 tablespoons heavy cream

Blend together the pumpkin, milk, eggs, and spices. Pour into prepared pie crust. Bake in Dutch oven at 350°F for about 1 hour. Sprinkle pecans on top. Mix remaining ingredients and bring to a boil in a separate pan. Reduce heat and simmer for about 5 minutes. Let cool a short while and spoon onto pie.

PHYLLIS SPEER
Mountain Home, Arizona

John Woodman's Cake

Use an 8-inch Dutch oven, and add a can of pie filling to the bottom, juice and all (cherry, apple, pineapple, peach, whatever you like). Then take a box of white cake mix, any brand, and dump it loose and dry over the whole mix below. Lay on four or five pats of butter on top of the dry mix. Cook on briquettes, eight below the pot, twelve on the lid. When the steam starts to flow out from under the lid it is done. That formula, eight briquettes below the pot and twelve on the lid, keeps the oven a near 400°F for an hour. For bigger ovens use the number on the lid, which is the diameter of the oven, to know how many briquettes to use. A 12-inch Dutch oven needs twelve briquettes under it and eighteen on top.

The juice of the can of fruit is pulled up into the dry cake mix, and it turns out very nice, like an apple strudel. This recipe is from John Woodman of Roseburg, Oregon.

HARLAN WHITE
Canyonville, Oregon

What's to Eat?
Staying Healthy in Camp

BY BILL ROMPA

In the early 1970s my partner Jake and I hunted out of his dad's mountain cabin in northeastern Oregon. His mom would come up with us, and when we rolled out of our bunk beds in the morning, there were biscuits and gravy, eggs, hash browns, bacon, sausage, and fresh, hot coffee waiting. She made and packed our lunches and filled our thermos with hot coffee.

When we returned with elk meat and were out back skinning and butchering, there were clean towels, soap, and hot water waiting inside the cabin for us. Each evening the aroma of fresh-baked chicken, roast beef, or ham filled the cabin. And there was always dessert after dinner. I especially remember the applesauce cake Jake's mom made, topped with home-canned peaches, pears, or apricots. We were spoiled rotten.

But there came a time for me to strike out and start my own elk camp. For several years, hunting with other friends, I slept on frozen ground in backpacking tents and cooked over a two-burner, white-gas camp stove. Brewing coffee and heating water for hot instant breakfast cereal when the pitch-dark morning air was 10°F got old in a real hurry. The last straw came when an unexpected storm dumped 15 inches of snow that caved in one of our tents as we slept. I decided then that the days of diarrhea, headache, constipation, dehydration, and complete exhaustion in our makeshift elk camps had to end. If I was to get serious about elk hunting and take better care of my campmates and myself, there simply had to be a better way.

During the next few years, I worked with a passion to find hunting partners willing to make the investment in gear and provisions for a proper elk camp. I obtained a small, single-axle camp trailer that could be used as a cook shack. My partners invested in several large tents equipped with wood stoves that provided reasonable protection from the harsh elements. We also began to take more care in meal planning and preparation.

We liked to hunt hard, and if we ate well and took better care of ourselves, I surmised, we could go for a week or more of intensive hunting and not feel exhausted after two or three days. As we made improvements, not only did we all feel better physically and mentally, but we also had more fun. Even when the hunting was slow and our meat poles were empty, at least we had the memories of elk camp meals and camaraderie to carry us through to next year.

BREAKFAST

To me, breakfast is always the most difficult meal. On most mornings we leave at least one or two hours before daybreak. Variables such as hunting pressure, weather, feed, and water conditions from day to day dictate the location of the animals we're after, and we may need to drive an hour or more from camp just to get to a trailhead, top of a ridge, or canyon where we will hunt. It is most important to get everyone fed and out of camp without wasting time.

After a couple days of hunting I feel groggy, sore, and tired when the alarm sounds at 3 A.M., and I would just as soon stay in the sack and let someone else cook. To ease the pain, a little preparation, planning, and routine helps immensely. I prepare the twenty-cup coffeepot the night before, use throwaway paper filters in the percolator for ease in cleanup, and find the premeasured coffee packets handy. All I have to do is roll out of my sleeping bag and light the burner under the prepared pot.

Our base camps for both deer and elk hunting are between 4,000 and 5,000 feet. At those elevations it takes at least forty-five minutes for a twenty-cup pot to boil. If the morning menu calls for any kind of meat to be cooked, I start right after the burner is lit under the coffee. A pound of bacon, for example, takes about a half hour to cook in a deep-rimmed frying pan. As the meat or other fixings are completed, I wrap them in sheets of aluminum foil and place them in a warm oven casserole. Not everyone eats at the same time in the morning. As the crew rises they can help themselves to a warm breakfast from the oven or side plate of the wood stove.

While not all-inclusive, a sample breakfast menu for a week of hunting is as follows:

Day 1: Blueberry pancakes, sausage links, applesauce, maple and berry syrup, homemade freezer strawberry jam, and peanut butter.

Day 2: Scrambled eggs, bacon, hash browns, toast, and jelly.

Day 3: French toast, ham steaks, canned fruit, maple and berry syrup, and peanut butter.

Day 4: Canned beef hash topped with poached eggs and shredded cheddar cheese, toast, and jelly.

Day 5: Sausage and ham with fried eggs on English muffins with a slice of cheddar cheese and hash brown cakes.

Day 6: Hot or cold cereal (oatmeal, wheat hearts, raisin bran, granola, or shredded wheat), bananas or canned fruit (peaches, pears, fruit cocktail, applesauce), with fried deer or elk backstrap or tenderloins and muffins.

Day 7: Egg omelet with chopped peppers, onions, celery, cubed ham, and shredded cheddar cheese, Polish or German sausage, toast, and jelly.

A two-burner, nonstick aluminum griddle can ease the pain and speed the process in preparing many breakfast meals. Fresh or canned juice, nonfat skim milk, hot cocoa, herb tea, and coffee are available with all breakfasts. Skim milk, with its absence of fat, will keep from spoiling in camp days longer than other varieties. I keep ½-gallon cartons of milk chilled in my camper propane refrigerator.

LUNCH

Lunch usually consists of a hoagie roll with mustard, a sealed two-and-a-half-ounce package of pressed luncheon meat, two individually wrapped cheese slices, a handful of baby carrots, a banana, an apple, and a package of cookies inside a gallon resealable plastic bag to be carried inside the backpack. Packing the lunch meat and cheese separately until lunchtime prevents soggy sandwiches. I carry one or two quarts of water, a soda, a sports drink, or a pouch of fruit juice. The remainder of my backpack consists of snacks: candy and granola bars, boxed raisins, trail mix, and dried fruit and nuts. If we plan to leave camp very early in the morning, we prepare lunches and load backpacks the previous night.

On most hunts we're gone all day and often do not get back to the pickup until dark. By that time we've usually consumed everything in our packs and arrive hungry and thirsty. So we keep two well-stocked coolers in the rig. One "wet cooler" contains sodas, canned juice, sports drinks, bottled water, cheese sticks, fresh fruits and vegetables, or iced breakfast leftovers. We also have a five-gallon canister of drinking water. The "dry cooler" contains snacks such as mixed nuts, crackers, canned fish (salmon, sardines) or processed meat, bread rolls, pickles and peppers, granola and candy bars, or homemade cookies and nut breads.

In the event we are in camp for the afternoon doing chores or resting, the following items are popular for lunch:

• Chili topped with shredded cheddar cheese, plus crackers or bread rolls, carrot or celery sticks, and apple slices.

• Turkey noodle soup topped with Parmesan cheese, crackers or bread rolls with grilled cheese sandwiches.

• Baked beans with ham pieces, crackers or bread rolls, carrot or celery sticks, and apple slices.

DINNER

Our crew tends to hunt hard and take advantage of every available day on the hunting season docket. For example, Oregon's first season, a lottery permit hunt for Rocky Mountain bull elk, is only five days long. More days than not we return to a cold, dark camp at least one hour after nightfall. Although everyone is hungry, enthusiastic volunteers in preparing dinner are often scarce. To help ease this problem, we have developed at least a partial solution: We prepare and freeze some of our dinner meals at home before the hunting season, then reheat them in camp. The propane oven in my camper works well for reheating the following dinners:

Day 1: Roast turkey, stove-top dressing, peas and corn or green beans, and whole wheat rolls.

Day 2: Baked Italian sausage lasagna, mixed bag salad, and warm garlic bread.

Day 3: Turkey enchiladas, Mexican rice, and refried beans topped with cheddar cheese.

Day 4: Meat and vegetable stew with biscuit dumplings.

Day 5: Baked or barbecued chicken, boiled rice or potatoes, and cole slaw.

Day 6: Baked Italian sausage links in spaghetti sauce, mostaccioli noodles, mixed bag salad, and warm garlic bread.

Day 7: Swiss steak with mushrooms and gravy, boiled or mashed potatoes, canned corn or green beans, and bread rolls.

Most of those dinners can be ready to serve one or two hours from the time we return to camp. An initial oven temperature of 350°F should be reduced to 300°F after the first hour to avoid burning the dinner. Still-frozen dinners, of course, take longer. Thawing the meal ahead of time can prevent complaints from hungry hunters waiting for dinner to be served.

Our standard dinner dessert is apple pie. I never leave home without at least two or three frozen apple pies. Cherry, pumpkin cream cheese, and pecan pies also go over well in camp. Toward the end of a hunt we may be down to serving walnut brownies, cookies, or other cakes for dessert, but the memory of those apple pies lingers.

HELPFUL TIPS

While preparing and freezing food at home is a great help in feeding hungry camp-mates, transporting and safely storing it for a week or longer can be a challenge. This is particularly true on early-season hunts when the weather is warm. To alleviate the problem, I exclusively use white "marine" coolers for storing and transporting frozen and refrigerated foods. The regular coolers are good for storing dry and canned goods or other supplies and provisions and keeping bugs and camp mice at bay, but they do not retard thawing as well as the marine coolers. I double- or even triple-wrap some home-cooked foods, first in aluminum foil, then in sealable freezer bags, then in white freezer paper, depending on the item. The packages are labeled with a grease pencil and are frozen hard for at least three days before leaving for camp. I surround the frozen packages in the coolers with eight- or twelve-cup plastic juice bottles of frozen water and then top the packed coolers with crushed and cubed ice to the brim before leaving town. Items that will be used first are placed on top. Once the coolers are sealed, I refrain from opening them until an item is needed, and I never drain the melted ice water. Keeping coolers covered with tarps or old sleeping bags and in the shade during the warmest and sunniest parts of the day also retards thawing dramatically. On a recent antelope hunt we kept food items at least partially frozen in camp for five days, even though daytime temperatures reached or exceeded 90°F on several days.

Buying items in bulk before the hunting season not only saves money but can also provide higher-quality provisions. I purchase, for example, a whole seven-and-a-half-pound side of thick-sliced quality bacon on sale and repackage it into four or five packages for use during hunting season. Chicken, sausages, hamburger, and other food items can be purchased at discount stores and processed in the same way. Slicing, shredding, and repackaging a two-pound brick of cheese at home in advance is economical and convenient, and helps keep the camp tidy.

I also combine one major food item to make two or more meals. For example, I roast a whole, unstuffed twenty-pound turkey at home. I divide the cooked sections of breast, leg, and thigh meat into packages wrapped in aluminum foil and freeze it for reheating in camp. The roasted back and wing sections can be boiled with onions, carrots, and celery for one hour, and the usable meat stripped from the bones to make turkey chili and enchiladas. The degreased broth can be used for soup. Similarly, I roast a ten-pound or larger ham shank and carve the meat as thick steaks for breakfast or thin slices for sandwiches. I use the bone and meat trimmings from the ham in homemade baked beans.

Cooking for large groups in camp can be tedious. Several years ago we had nine hungry mouths to feed in elk camp. To help ease the strain of tight quarters and to save time, we broke into two groups and prepared and served our meals in two places. Everyone was happy and well fed.

One of the biggest problems I've seen and experienced myself in hunting camp is dehydration. To avoid dehydration, I often place a thirty-two-ounce plastic cup for drinking water inside my trailer the first few days in camp and challenge myself to see how many refills I can down in a day. I also do my part in nagging everyone in camp to drink more water.

While I'm not a teetotaler, I have learned over years of hunting camps gone by to go easy on the consumption of alcohol, especially during the first several days in camp. While we enjoy beer, wine, and hard liquor in our camp, most of us limit ourselves to two or three drinks per night.

One year I experienced a severe bout of food poisoning from eating and cooking with unsanitary utensils. The accompanying nausea, diarrhea, and headache entirely ruined the better part of a quality hunting trip. To avoid these conditions, we often use disposable paper plates, plastic silverware, and drinking cups. All other cooking and eating utensils are completely sanitized with hot, soapy water and thoroughly rinsed before reuse.

Traveling from just above sea level at home to a base camp at 4,000 to 5,000 feet in twelve hours, combined with all the excitement of an upcoming hunt, places a tremendous strain on the human body. We often need several days to acclimate to these changes and may feel nauseated during that time. Good, fresh, appealing food helps us recover more quickly.

Most of what my partners and I have learned has come by trial and error. Before using a meal or technique in camp, I usually practice at home until I get it right. Mistakes can be composted or fed to the dogs. Reading a lot of cookbooks and experimenting with various recipes also helps.

Each year I like to try cooking something new. Several years ago I made pies in camp from scratch. Although I originally thought it would be a big hassle, the pies turned out well and it was not that big a chore. This year I received one of those bread-making machines as a Christmas present. It works well and the bread tastes pretty good fresh and warm right from the machine. I plan to bake some garlic bread in camp this year from scratch. We'll see how it goes. One of these days my partners and I may be as spoiled as Jake and I were back when his mother cooked for us in that old cabin in northeastern Oregon.

Bill Rompa lives in Albany, Oregon. He has hunted elk and deer in Oregon and Washington for more than twenty-five years.

Chronic Wasting Disease: Recommendations for Hunters

BY THE CWD ALLIANCE

With the growing media attention given to Chronic Wasting Disease, many hunters are asking if they should continue to hunt in areas where CWD has been identified and to eat the deer and elk they harvest from those areas. In parts where CWD occurs, only a relatively small number of animals are affected. Even in the parts of Wyoming and Colorado where CWD has existed for at least thirty years, an average of less than 6 percent of deer are infected. Infection rates in affected deer herds in Colorado vary from less than 1 percent to 13 percent. CWD is far less prevalent in elk than deer. Less than 1 percent of elk found in areas where the disease occurs in northeastern Colorado are infected.

There is currently no scientific evidence that CWD has or can spread to humans, either through contact with infected animals or by eating meat of infected animals. The Centers for Disease Control have thoroughly investigated any connection between CWD and the human forms of TSEs (transmissible spongiform encephalopathies) and stated, "The risk of infection with the CWD agent among hunters is extremely small, if it exists at all," and, "It is extremely unlikely that CWD would be a food-borne hazard."

However, public health officials advise caution and recommend that human exposure to the CWD infectious agent be avoided as they continue to evaluate any potential health risk. Hunters are encouraged not to consume meat from animals known to be infected with CWD. In addition, hunters should take certain precautions when field dressing and processing deer or elk taken in areas where CWD is found.

SIMPLE PRECAUTIONS ADVISED

Public health and wildlife officials advise hunters to take the following precautions when pursuing or handling deer and elk that may have been exposed to CWD:

- Do not shoot, handle, or consume any animal that is acting abnormally or appears to be sick. Contact your state game and fish department if you see or harvest an animal that appears sick.
- Wear latex or rubber gloves when field dressing your deer or elk.
- Bone out the meat from your animal. Don't saw through bone, and avoid cutting through the brain or spinal cord (backbone).
- Minimize the handling of brain and spinal tissues.
- Wash hands and instruments thoroughly after field dressing is completed.
- Avoid consuming brain, spinal cord, eyes, spleen, tonsils, and lymph nodes of harvested animals. (Normal field dressing coupled with boning out a carcass will remove most, if not all, of these body parts. Cutting away all fatty tissue will remove remaining lymph nodes.)
- Avoid consuming the meat from any animal that tests positive for the disease.
- If you have your deer or elk commercially processed, request that your animal is processed individually, without meat from other animals being added to meat from your animal.
- The Wisconsin Department of Agriculture, Trade, and Consumer Protection has developed a brochure on field dressing and processing deer. This excellent resource can be found on the Web at http://datcp.state.wi.us/ah/agriculture/animals/disease/chronic/pdf/venison_safety_2side.pdf.

For more information, visit the CWD Alliance Web site at www.cwd-info.org.

RECIPE INDEX

C